Managing Intellectual Capital in Libraries

CHANDOS
INFORMATION PROFESSIONAL SERIES

Series Editor: Ruth Rikowski
(e-mail: Rikowskigr@aol.com)

Chandos' new series of books is aimed at the busy information professional. They have been specially commissioned to provide the reader with an authoritative view of current thinking. They are designed to provide easy-to-read and (most importantly) practical coverage of topics that are of interest to librarians and other information professionals. If you would like a full listing of current and forthcoming titles, please visit www. chandospublishing.com or e-mail wp@woodheadpublishing.com or telephone +44(0) 1223 499140

New authors: we are always pleased to receive ideas for new titles; if you would like to write a book for Chandos, please contact Dr Glyn Jones on e-mail gjones@chandospublishing. com or telephone +44 (0) 1993 848726.

Bulk orders: some organisations buy a number of copies of our books. If you are interested in doing this, we would be pleased to discuss a discount. Please contact on e-mail wp@woodheadpublishing.com or telephone +44(0) 1223 499140.

Managing Intellectual Capital in Libraries

Beyond the balance sheet

PETROS KOSTAGIOLAS

CP

CHANDOS
PUBLISHING

Oxford Cambridge Philadelphia New Delhi

Chandos Publishing
Hexagon House
Avenue 4
Station Lane
Witney
Oxford OX28 4BN
UK
Tel: +44 (0) 1993 848726
E-mail: info@chandospublishing.com
www.chandospublishing.com

Chandos Publishing is an imprint of Woodhead Publishing Limited

Woodhead Publishing Limited
80 High Street
Sawston, Cambridge CB22 3HJ
UK
Tel: +44 (0) 1223 499140
Fax: +44 (0) 1223 832819
www.woodheadpublishing.com

First published in 2012

ISBN: 978-1-84334-678-4 (print)
ISBN: 978-1-78063-315-2 (online)

British Library Cataloguing-in-Publication Data.
A catalogue record for this book is available from the British Library.

Typeset by RefineCatch Ltd, Bungay, Suffolk.

To my beloved baby girl Mary,
an intellectual capital heritage for her future quests

Contents

List of figures

List of tables

List of abbreviations

ACRL	Association of College and Research Libraries
AHP	Analytic Hierarchy Process
ALA	American Library Association
ARCS	Austrian Research Centers Seibersdorf
ARL	Association of Research Libraries
BSC	Balanced Scorecard
BV	book value
cdf	cumulative distribution function
CH	Cumulative-Hazard
chf	cumulative hazard function
CoP	Community of Practice
CRM	Customer Relationship Management
CSF	Critical Success Factors
DIC	Direct Intellectual Capital methods
DMSTI	Danish Ministry of Science, Technology and Innovation
EU	European Union
FI	Financial Indicator
GOF	Goodness Of Fit
HC	human capital
IAS	International Accounting Standards
IC	intellectual capital
ICT	information and communication technology
iid	independent and identically distributed
IT	Information Technology
KM	Kaplan-Meier
LCA	Library Copyright Alliance

MAVT   Multi-Attribute Value Theory
MCM   Market Capitalization Methods
MERITUM   MEasuRing Intangibles To Understand and
              improve innovation Management
MLE   Maximum Likelihood Estimation
MMR   mixed method research
MV   monetary value
NFI   Non-Financial Indicator
OA   Open Access
OC   organizational capital
OECD   Organization for Economic Co-operation and
              Development
OPAC   online public access catalog
OSS   Open Source Software
pdf   probability density function
PL   Product–Limit
PLACE   Public Libraries—Arenas for Citizenship
PV   physical value
PWC   pair-wise comparisons
R&D   Research and Development
RC   relational capital
ROA   Return On Assets
ROI   Return On Investment
SC   structural capital
SCCR   Standing Committee on Copyright and
              Related Rights
STM   Scientific, Technical, and Medical
TBL   Triple Bottom Line
TSER   Targeted Socio-Economic Research
VAIC™   Value-Added Intellectual Coefficient
VHD   Virtual Help Desks
WCT   World Copyright Treaty
WIPO   World Intellectual Property Organization

Foreword

This book is a most welcomed addition to the literature of librarianship. It brings a fresh approach to past efforts that have tried to prove the value of libraries. Recently, there have been efforts through associations and by individual libraries to identify the financial and economic benefit they produce for their communities. Over decades, the field developed increasingly sophisticated performance measures using metrics and other tools. More recently, governments, foundations, and taxpayers have demanded outcome information instead of outputs such as circulation data. Simply put, funding agencies want to know the impact of their financial support on end users. They want to understand how the lives of program participants have improved as a result of a program or operation. In order to articulate outcomes, libraries have had to learn to reassess assumptions about end users' needs and desires, prepare statements that indicate the purpose of their operation, define inputs (tangibles such as books), articulate the activities to be undertaken, and list the outputs (for example, numbers of individuals participating in a training event). The most difficult part of this assessment process was to determine *outcomes*, namely how the program/project/ operations have altered or improved the knowledge, skills, attitudes, and behavior of clients served by an organization.

Beginning in 2008 when the global fiscal meltdown began, libraries began to experience even more pressure to prove their value at all levels—more than outcomes can provide. Dr. Kostagiolas gives readers a path to meet these growing demands by describing how libraries can identify, quantify, manage, measure, and calculate the value of their intellectual capital. He takes a logical and thorough approach to translating how intangible assets can be identified in library environments. He presents definitions and the fundamentals of intellectual capital, followed by a framework for libraries to use. He not only describes how libraries can identify various intangible assets, but also outlines metrics and other tools that can be used to measure intellectual capital in libraries. He provides three approaches for identifying and presenting the value of libraries' intangible assets: cost, market, and income. Finally he discusses management of intellectual capital from the perspective of reliability and longevity, providing methods for analysis of these.

As he points out, previous research efforts about intellectual capital as an intangible asset have been largely in sectors other than libraries. His translation of this body of work into library environments provides the field with yet another means to report their value to stakeholders. Library literature about identifying and managing intellectual capital is scarce. Therefore this book provides a solid intellectual contribution to our literature. More than that, it gives librarians everywhere not just an analysis and synthesis of the topic, but also frameworks for implementing them. When libraries are able to articulate their intangible assets, they will have tools and strategies to strengthen their position in a competitive information/knowledge environment. Dr. Kostagiolas' thorough research and his analysis of the existing literature on the topic makes this book one that should be added to all discipline-based collections, not only those about librarianship.

Anne Woodsworth, Ph.D.
Glen Cove, NY, USA
September 2011

Preface

Economies and societies should focus on intellectual capital resources at the center of changes mainly arising from innovative information, communication technologies, and the Internet. As a matter of fact, organizations and enterprises around the world are based more and more on intellectual capital, while their sustainability depends upon its successful utilization. Libraries create and, at the same time, utilize intellectual capital. The paradox is that in many cases intellectual capital resources which seem to be essential for the knowledge economy are often treated as the "Cinderella" of resources, holding an unclear role. Although libraries have changed markedly over the past decades, it is now time for library professionals to face "intellectual capital management" systematically and consciously. Intellectual capital resources should be managed properly so as to be identified and categorized, their quality and quantity should be measured throughout their entire lifecycle and they should be financially valuated. The stakes are high for librarians and information scientists, who are expected to prove their value within harsh economic circumstances faced by most societies around the world.

Intellectual capital has become the buzzword of a knowledge-based economy and is the ultimate source of competitive advantage for libraries. Intellectual capital-based library management is gradually becoming a crucial issue fostering innovation that genuinely improves library operations, services, and relations. On the other hand, guidance is required as regards the utilization of library intellectual capital resources, understanding relations and patterns, etc. In this context, a systematic approach towards the study of library intellectual capital is definitely required. The development of intellectual capital resources should be viewed as a key aspect of every library's strategy. Such a strategy may involve the development of best practices so that specific tangible or intangible resources are not isolated but organized and managed within a holistic framework. This book is addressed to library practitioners and academics of all levels who want to venture into the exciting area of intellectual capital management in libraries, and it will attempt to increase their awareness by providing relevant examples together with analytical management methods and techniques. Being a novel and multifaceted subject, the management of intellectual capital in libraries is a challenging and very interesting area of research.

The book covers a number of important and interrelated issues as regards library intellectual capital management. Chapter 1 touches upon the concepts and fundamentals of intellectual capital and its significance within the dynamics of the knowledge economy, analyzing issues of identification and categorization. Chapter 2 provides a historical perspective on intellectual capital utilization in libraries through the Worlds of Production framework. Chapter 3 presents metrics and measurement methods, methodologically linking the availability of intangibles in terms of their quality and quantity with the library's ability to reach long-term aims. Chapter 4 analyzes financial valuation and reporting methods for library intellectual resources, while Chapter 5 includes methods and techniques for assessing life characteristics and conducting parametric or nonparametric life analysis modeling for intellectual capital resources in libraries. Finally, Chapter 6 summarizes in a synthesized manner the different methods and techniques for library intellectual capital, and provides thoughts for further research on this innovative and exciting area of library management.

Petros A. Kostagiolas, Ph.D.
Ionian University, Greece
October 2011

Acknowledgements

The research on library intellectual capital, as on any other field, should be developed, established, and finally made public after engaging in an active dialog with colleagues, researchers, and students. Apart from colleagues in Greece from the Ionian University, the University of Athens, the University of Piraeus, and the Hellenic Open University, who have shared with me certain issues for intellectual capital management at times, my students have heavily contributed to the promotion of the main research idea of this book and I would like to thank them wholeheartedly. I would mostly like to thank the postgraduate students at the Ionian University, Department of Archives and Library Science, and especially graduate and mathematician Mr Stefanos Asonitis, with whom I have worked closely over the past few years and written publications on the subject. I would also like to acknowledge the significant help of Ms Marilleia Tilli for achieving a smooth and creative transition of some coursework material and texts from Greek to English, with kindness and talent. As regards the endorsement of this publication, final proofreading and copy-editing, I would like to thank Chandos Publishing for their excellent cooperation.

A special reference should be made to Professor Anne Woodsworth, who has encouraged me in many ways during the creation of the book, contributing with useful comments and creative remarks, and honoring me with a foreword to this edition. Professor Woodsworth is currently Editor at Advances in Librarianship, former Provost and Dean at the

Pratt Institute, Dean of the Palmer School of Library and Information Science at Long Island University, Associate Provost and Director of Libraries at the University of Pittsburgh and the York University in Toronto, Canada, specializing in higher education and libraries with emphasis on strategic planning, library management, professional development, outcomes-based evaluation/assessment, project management, and assessing the needs for facility planning.

About the author

Dr. Petros A. Kostagiolas holds a Ph.D. in reliability management from the University of Birmingham, UK. He had received a full scholarship (fees and maintenance) during his research studies (1995–99) from the University of Birmingham.

Since 2007, he has been a full-time staff member (lecturer) on information services management at the Department of Archives and Library Science, Ionian University, Greece. At the Ionian University he teaches library and archives management, museum management, quality management, human resources management, and social research methods. Petros Kostagiolas also teaches management, quality, and reliability management in postgraduate courses at the University of Athens and the University of Piraeus, and since 2003 he has been tutoring on a postgraduate management course at the Faculty of Social Sciences of the Hellenic Open University.

Petros Kostagiolas has been a co-author of four other books and has published his work as chapters in international edited books (*Advances in Librarianship Book Series*, etc.), international journals (*Health Information and Libraries Journal, International Journal of Management Concepts and Philosophy, Library Management, Library Review, New Library World, The Journal of Hospital Librarianship*, etc.), and conference proceedings (*Conference of Operation Research Society U.K., Conference on Qualitative and Quantitative Methods in Libraries, European Conference of*

Medical and Health Libraries, International Conference on Electronic Publishing, International Conference on Typography and Visual Communication, etc.). He has published material and presentations on a number of topics including library and information services management, intellectual capital management, publishing, knowledge revolution and the new economy, information-seeking behavior, quality management, and reliability management. He has been a member of a number of professional and scientific societies and associations, while he is a reviewer for a number of journals and conferences.

Petros, over the past 15 years, has been involved in a number of research and professional projects with a range of organizations, in both the public and the private sectors. In particular, he has experience in regard to operations and quality management, long-term planning, information services development, intellectual capital applications, studies on the contributions of information services to their environment, and lifelong learning programs.

Over the past ten years he has settled on the island of Corfu, in north-western Greece, near the University premises, with his wife Christina Banou, their beautiful baby girl Mary, his immediate family, and friends. Still, he is spending most of his time at the university with his students, writing and . . . working with a hope that it can all have some actual impact on society and the economy, given the fact that today, the economic crisis in Greece and globally is severe.

Petros Kostagiolas can be contacted at *pkostagiolas@ ionio.gr*

Libraries in the knowledge economy: introducing intellectual capital concepts

Abstract: The discussion begins with a definition and a classification of intangible assets as well as an identification of a number of innovative and interesting issues concerning library intellectual capital management. This chapter will mainly deal with the following issues.

- How is intellectual capital defined and what might be its significance for library management?
- What has been reported in the literature as regards library intellectual capital?
- What is library intellectual capital management?

Intellectual capital management in libraries comprises methods and practices for identifying and developing intellectual capital. The intellectual capital used or produced by libraries goes beyond the balance sheet and captures true library value.

Key words: knowledge economy, intellectual capital, intangible assets, value, library management.

Introduction: libraries within the knowledge-driven economy

In the second decade of the 21st century, the global economy functions quite differently than it did in the previous century, mainly due to the way intellectual capital is utilized. Within this new economic environment, data, information, and knowledge are considered to be essential factors for decision making (Drucker, 2008). There is no doubt that intangible assets have become vital for organizations and enterprises these days. Intellectual capital is enhancing overall business performance, innovativeness, and the total assets held by any organization. Now more than ever, the unrestricted flow of information within or around organizations and enterprises is becoming essential (Burke, 2011). This, however, expands beyond the mere implementation of information and communication technologies, and should include properly designed management structures in order for organizations to make the most of all their available intangible assets. The development of information-based organizations lies in specifying management practices and more particularly in certain processes that utilize intellectual capital and generate value. The intricacy is that the management of most organizations does not quite recognize the significance of the existing links of their processes with intellectual capital.

The increased availability in information technologies does not imply free information and knowledge sharing. This can easily be explained if one considers that the more information and knowledge are linked to specific functions and jobs within an organization, the more they are considered as a source of power and hence they are not expected to be shared freely within or outside the organization. In the knowledge economy, however, the accumulation of information and knowledge is considered to be more important than the actual physical capital. Within this context, the management of information and knowledge, knowledge sharing, as well as the management of intellectual capital assets, become a rather important issue. Managing efficiently and effectively in order to create intellectual capital has become the holy grail of academics and practitioners, and is at the center of all knowledge economy discussions.

Societies and economies can be viewed as living entities that are constantly changing and developing new cultural and socioeconomic needs throughout different periods. Over the years, many changes have taken place and the certainties of each time period were replaced by new ones leading to new structures, relations, and communication means. The history of libraries, parallel to the history of the human kind, provides examples of such changes under the pressure of social shifts, technological advances, and the development of human knowledge and science. Of course, the changes taking place in societies as a whole can also be observed within individual organizations and enterprises. Although libraries preserve many of their basic cultural foundations, they are constantly changing and "moving" to new structures with new operations and services. Nowadays, the rapid development of information technologies and the Internet are the main drivers of change. The burgeoning of innovative information and communication technologies (ICTs) and the expansion of the Internet provide an extensive variety of information and knowledge management tools, while information and knowledge are now more accessible than ever before. Within this context of significant changes, libraries as part of societies and economies can be viewed in two ways.

1. Libraries operate within a socioeconomic environment that utilizes their intellectual capital and library

professionals all over the world strive to redefine their role and develop innovative systems and services in order to contribute to the development of services and relationships. Hence, libraries can be viewed as important intellectual capital "creators", either within wider organizations (e.g. academic libraries, hospital libraries) or within society and economy as a whole (e.g. public libraries).

2. Even if we do not directly realize it, when we use libraries as part of our daily practice we rely heavily upon intangible assets. Intellectual capital is gradually becoming a crucial element for the development and sustainability of libraries, fostering innovation and genuinely improving operations and services. Intellectual capital includes the total of intangible assets (and resources)—that is to say, the invisible, non-monetary assets held by a library, which can be identified and analyzed individually. Some library administration and management decisions include investments in intangible assets in the form of technological/structural, organizational, and/or human capital. These assets need to be identified and measured properly in order to understand fully their possible uses, structure, production, and value.

For individual society members or organizations, socioeconomic changes are not directly perceptible and thus there might be a delay between their incidence and the effects they have on society. This means that individuals tend to adapt to new organizational frameworks more slowly. Human organizational behaviors and particularities put yet another obstacle in the way of intellectual capital management. Incorporating this new factor, management science is no longer restricted to a merely passive study of social demands and developments, but is beginning to research organizational issues and human behaviors within organizations, providing its own estimations and variables. Library management is expected to internalize and take into consideration socioeconomic "certainties" as developed through time. Intellectual capital management is a key factor for the structuring and operation of 21st century libraries.

Rapid developments in technologies and ICTs, telecommunications and the Internet are causing radical global changes, restructuring the distribution of values throughout library production factors. In this context, we should realize that any change in social organization or the way of producing or thinking and acting occurs in two stages: first, there is a change in structures and means of production, which leads to the formulation of novel library management theories, and then the behavior of individuals (e.g. professionals) is adjusted to them. This transition process is not easy, and is rarely smooth. Library professionals, who have learned to work in certain ways, are called to follow new workflows, roles, information uses, social relations, and contacts. This is a time-consuming process, demanding a change in mentality, behavior, and stance. It is not a transition that occurs effortlessly, just because the new paradigm might be more effective. In any kind of change, mobilizing the human factor is the hardest and most time-consuming step, calling for an initial research and understanding of behaviors and stances (differentiated for each social or professional group), then assuming the necessary action so as to convince individuals or groups to alter their behavior.

When deciding to change direction, human behaviors and stances cannot be convinced to change automatically. This is also the case for library management. Library members, just like society members, initially adopt a cautious stance towards the changes proposed by a library management theory and need time to adapt to new administrative practices. This procedure is not effortless and requires an adaptation period so as to achieve a comprehensive acceptance of administrational practices. This means that in order for management actions or proposals to be effective, they need to be more or less legitimized by a theory, i.e. a library management paradigm, and empirical evidence. This is the case of the intellectual capital management paradigm in libraries. Based on the above-mentioned facts it is clear that, both at the financial and organizational level, established relations (that is, the way individuals or organizations communicate and contact each other) are hard to change since the members of each large or small group need time to familiarize themselves with new tools and conditions. In this context, this book aims to analyze management practices and decision making for libraries based on an understanding of the effect that the intellectual capital has on this particular field, taking into account its particularities. It is extremely important that any management approach should not be isolated from the wider socioeconomic conditions, while taking into account and fully understanding the particularities of the field. The present work is supported by the following interrelated assumptions.

1. Intellectual capital is a crucial element for libraries, fostering innovation and genuine improvements in library operation and services.

2. The library environment is becoming more and more complicated and knowledge based, hence conventional instruments are no longer directly appropriate for decision making.

3. Expenditures and investments in intellectual capital are either mis-measured or not measured at all.

Intellectual capital: fundamental concepts and definitions

Over the past decades, many library management paradigms have developed for a number of reasons including technological advances (e.g. advances in information and communication technologies, new distribution networks, and the Internet), organizational restructuring (for example quality assurance, collaborations), increasing market competition (for example globalization), new legislation (for example development of the European Union), etc. A new economic environment is unfolding and evolving, while bringing about changes by developing, maintaining, and withdrawing services in libraries (Walton, 2007). Understanding and managing the intellectual capital of libraries within this new and highly competitive information environment is essential since conventional capital alone is no longer a sufficient condition for success. The present economic recession is affecting library funding on a global level and is putting forward the need for utilizing the intellectual capital used or produced by libraries (Kostagiolas et al., 2011).

There is little agreement as to whether "intellectual capital" consists of assets[1] with some researchers preferring the term "resources." In fact, according to some researchers, intangibles cannot be always owned by an organization but only used by it, so they cannot be defined as "assets"—at least in the economic sense. In this work, unless specified for a particular intangible or for a particular methodology, the terms "assets" and "resources" will be used interchangeably. Nevertheless, intellectual capital is considered to be an important factor (group of assets or resources) that can play a significant part in improving productivity, efficiency, effectiveness, and quality in any organization (Ark, 2002). Libraries are actually turning intellectual capital into an

7

economic and cultural advantage, providing individual users with more choices. Libraries contribute to their social environment, systems, or organizations where they belong. Consider, for example, the Brooklyn Public Library projects for supporting learning and children (Woodsworth, 2005) or the Public Libraries—Arenas for Citizenship (PLACE) project (Ulvik, 2010) which aims to create social value by collecting immigrants' memories, at a public library in Oslo, Norway. We can assume that the vast majority of library professionals always were and still are, one way or another, aware of the significance of the library's value through exploitation of its intellectual capital. In fact, as opposed to traditional economic thinking, which does not include intellectual capital, it seems that a library culture based on the presence of a "different kind of capital" was diachronically present. This was and is in fact the intellectual capital used or produced by libraries.

Intellectual capital can be defined as the total of intangible assets—that is, all the invisible, non-monetary assets held by an organization that are amassed over time, not included in the balance sheet, and can be identified and analyzed separately. The term "intellectual capital" has been given different interpretations (Kaufman and Schneider, 2004). In economics, the term "knowledge asset" is commonly used as an equivalent for "intangible asset," while in the field of management the term "intellectual capital" is used quite extensively (Lev, 2001). The definitions provided for the term "intangible asset" and its equivalents may be either conceptual or descriptive (providing a list of assets or resources considered to be intangible). Examples of conceptual definitions are Lev's "an intangible asset is a claim to future benefit that does not have a physical or financial (a stock or a bond) embodiment" (Lev, 2001) and the one provided by Boutellier (2000), stressing that an intangible asset originates in "past events" not physical in nature, legally protected and capable of producing future economic benefits. Reilly and Schweihs (1998) provide a descriptive definition and record an indicative list of intangibles, including computer software and databases, patents, copyrights, trademarks, customer lists, applied marketing techniques, contracts with suppliers, etc. The total of intangible assets held by a firm or an organization constitutes their intellectual capital.

In order to better understand and recognize the intellectual capital of a library, a deconstruction of the definitions provided above might be quite useful and lead to an intellectual capital classification. The relevant literature includes quite a few efforts for the classification of intangible assets or intellectual capital (e.g. Reilly and Schweihs, 1998; Rodov and Leliart, 2002; Grasenick and Low, 2004; Kannan and Aulbur, 2004; Porta and Oliver, 2006; Choong, 2008). These classification methods usually set out a number of categories under which intangibles should be classified. Classifications may satisfy various research needs. For instance, some classifications might serve accounting practices or relate to the economic performance of intangibles. Reilly and Schweihs (1998) propose a classification method that promotes a valuation analysis. According to their classification, intangibles can fit into ten categories:

1. marketing
2. technology
3. art
4. data processing
5. engineering science
6. customers
7. obligations derived from contracts

8. human capital

9. locality

10. trademark.

Lev (2001) proposes an alternative classification according to the creator of each intangible asset, within or outside the organization. Other categorization approaches have been or may be further developed for specific sectors and/or industries or firm-specific categorizations, serving specific or internal analysis needs. For example, Porta and Oliver (2006) provide an analysis of intangibles within enterprise clusters, and a number of alternative classifications are provided in Chapters 4 and 5, together with the measurement and financial valuation methods.

A widely recognized categorization is presented in several academic papers published in the Journal of Intellectual Capital including those by Edvinsson and Malone (1997), Roos et al. (1997), Sveiby (1997), MERITUM (2002), Bontis (2002), Grasenick and Low (2004), Gallego and Rodríguez (2005). According to this approach, the intellectual capital can be classified into three distinct categories:

1. human capital

2. organizational (or structural) capital

3. relational capital.

An extensive analysis of the literature based on the classification presented above is provided by Choong (2008). Table 1.1 presents a synthesis of explanatory phrases for the meaning of the three intellectual capital categories.

Human capital includes the knowledge, experiences, competencies, and creativity of the staff working for a firm or an organization (Edvinsson and Malone, 1997). Resources related to human capital are closely linked to individuals and

Table 1.1 Explanatory phrases for the classification of intellectual capital

Categories of intellectual capital	Explanatory phrases
Human capital (HC)	Includes the knowledge, experiences, competencies and creativity of the staff Knowledge that employees take with them when they leave the firm Knowledge workers own the means of production—it is the knowledge between their ears, and it is a totally portable and enormous capital asset Constitutes the talent base of the personnel Is related to how effectively an organization uses its human resources, measured through creativity and innovation Human capability for resolving business problems Is related to individuals and cannot be replaced by machines
Organizational/ structural capital (OC/SC)	Infrastructure, processes, and databases of a library that enable the work of the human capital (e.g. the library collection and stocks, the organizational philosophy and structure, management systems (quality and safety management systems), automation and other information systems, patents, copyrights, etc.) Knowledge that stays within the firm at the end of the working day Non-human storehouses of information
Relational capital (RC)	Value created through relationships with the external environment and more specifically with investors and creditors Resources linked to the external relationships of the firm Value embedded in business networks Value of the brand name

cannot, in any case, be replaced by machines (Roos et al., 2005). Organizational or structural capital can be defined according to Edvinsson and Malone (1997) as "all those things that remain in the organization when the employees have left the building but that you cannot find in the balance sheet." These may include the organizational structure, management system, information systems (computer software and databases), patents, and copyrights owned by a firm or an organization. Relational capital (Grasenick and Low, 2004) can be defined as the value created through the relations that a firm or an organization holds with its external environment (i.e. providers, customers, potential customers, users, sellers, other firms and organizations). Relational capital is also linked to the value deriving from the relations that the firm or organization has with its stakeholders, investors, and creditors, as well as the value of its brand name.

Reviewing intellectual capital for libraries

In a pioneering work, Barron (1995) stressed the need for intellectual capital investments when considering staffing public libraries. A little later, Koeing (1997) argued that intellectual capital should be turned into a comparative advantage by librarians and pointed out the significance of measuring it. Annual reports presenting the current status of the utilization of library intellectual capital were suggested to be equally important as any other library report. As we will see further on, such a report should comprise a list of indicators that reflect the library's resources and investments in intellectual capital. For instance, within the relational capital category the loyalty of library users can be considered as an important intangible asset and may be expressed through an indicator of the percentage of active library users over a time period. Another intangible asset of the same category might include the relationships built with the publishers and could be measured through the number of active printed and digital library subscriptions. Proper management decisions could be based on annual reports that include intangible asset indicators. Dakers (1998) studied the importance of intellectual asset audits for personnel skills, ". . . the living intellectual capital of the British Library," as the author characteristically stated. The word "living" is used in order ". . . to distinguish between the intellectual capital produced by the British Library's own staff and that much greater part of it which is contained within its stock"—i.e. the structural capital of the British Library.

Rowley (1999) has also identified the potential of intellectual capital within libraries by managing knowledge as an asset and by recognizing its value within a library. The author identified "typical" knowledge assets (intangible assets) that are purchased under license and have a potential value or assets such as customer databases and detailed parts catalogs to which value can be assigned. The work of Portugal (2000) includes an extensive analysis of the significance of intellectual capital for libraries. Portugal (2000) also provides a review of four library measurement methods, one of which regards intellectual capital financial valuation. Innovation turns good ideas and opportunities into intellectual and social capital, through which new library services are being developed (Bryson, 2001). In order to mobilize the value of intellectual capital assets, a set of new skills is required on the part of the information professionals, together with a far greater focus on sharing and exchanging information across successful organizations (Todd and Southon, 2001; Pember, 2002).

Materska (2004) states that in this "network economy," network participation and the relationships involved are more significant than actually owning the assets. In the case of an academic library, this statement leads to the suggestion that "it is more preferable for an academic library to gain access rights for a document than to acquire the document itself." One of the four perspectives of the Bond University Library's Balanced Scorecard proposed by Cribb (2005) is "Learning and Growth." Zhang (2006) states that an accurate method to evaluate the intellectual property rights of a digital library is considering parameters such as contracts with the authors of electronic resources, copyrights, the size of the digitized collection, and access rules. Hood and Henderson (2005) point out the importance of including branding (a set of features that identify a provider of a good or service, among others) in public library marketing plans as a tool to improve the image of the library and reverse the negative perception users have of public library services in the UK. Sheng and Sun (2007) analyze some library assets, such as organizational structure (i.e. knowledge-based team organization), business processes, learning culture, administration systems, reputation, and the total of rules and regulations. All the assets mentioned above are examples of intangibles embodied in the organizational (or structural) capital of a library.

Sheng and Sun (2007) stressed that trust and cooperation can advance the development of human and relational capital: through trust and cooperation, library professionals share new knowledge and skills, contributing to an "improvement of the library's intellectual capital and staff capacity for solving problems and doing knowledge creation." Furthermore, trust and cooperation provide opportunities to build relations among libraries and between libraries and their users. Garnes (2007), through a review of Bergen University Library in Norway, suggests that the library handles information beyond its collection since it is managing the institution's entire intellectual capital. Thus, a development of the library's structural capital strategy is suggested and should be conducted through a digitalization of its unique and valuable collections in order to make them available for users. White (2007a) stated that the identification of intangible assets in a library provides three benefits for the management team:

1. the ability to present a report illustrating the library's effectiveness to stakeholders;

2. the ability to unify the library's tangible and intangible resources in order to meet the requirements of stakeholders;

3. the ability to utilize the library's intangibles in order to achieve its strategic objectives.

For this purpose, White (2007a) classified intellectual capital into customer (or relational) capital, human capital, and structural capital. The author concludes that "a library has multiple intangible assets, resources, and efforts that are not generally accounted for in traditional tangible assessments, accountability reporting, or budget planning," and there is a need to learn how to manage the intellectual capital used/produced by a library in order to increase the library's effectiveness by utilizing the library's inherent intangible assets and resources of information, knowledge, and services. In another work by the same author (White, 2007b), human capital was identified as a core element for assessing library performance. An effective human capital management could become a tool for decision making on budget allocation, recruitment, staff training, and library service improvements. In like manner, Livonen and Huotari (2007) analyzed the same three categories of intellectual capital (human, structural, and relational) within the context of an academic library. Among the intangible assets included in human capital are the knowledge, experience, capabilities, skills, and competencies of the staff. The staff's knowledge, skills, and competencies are further analyzed and explained through various examples. The intangible assets classified under structural capital include organizational structure, library systems, databases, content description, metadata, and access to information resources.

Livonen and Huotari (2007) have also pointed out that relational capital might include information literacy training programs, the relationships formed between the academic library and those in academia (for example, students, researchers, teachers), and other factors, such as cooperating with publishers. Other researchers have examined the relation between public libraries and social capital creation (Varheim, 2009), which may be considered as a component of the public structural capital according to the Intellectual Capital General Model for the public sector proposed by Bueno et al. (2003). Social capital developed by libraries (Bryson, 2001) contributes to preventative healthcare, fostering innovation and sustainability (Marcum, 2008), improving environmental management, developing more efficient transport systems, the use of renewable energy sources, understanding climate change, etc. In fact, the aforementioned model for the public sector includes the three main components of intellectual capital, namely public human capital, public structural capital, and public relational capital (Figure 1.1); however, public structural capital is

Figure 1.1 Relationship between intellectual capital and the creation of social capital through library operations and services

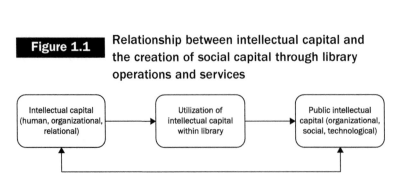

further divided into three components: public organizational capital, public social capital, and public technological capital.

This model has been employed to analyze the intellectual capital of the Spanish public sector (Ramirez, 2010). Corrall and Sriborisutsakul (2010) presented an explanatory analysis based on survey results from three academic libraries in Thailand. Their analysis aimed to develop indicators of intellectual capital assets and the related performance measures for evaluating library intangibles. Table 1.2

| **Table 1.2** | Indicative intangible assets for libraries and information services |

Intellectual capital category	Indicative intangible assets
Human capital (HC)	Staff training/education Staff quality/competence/skills/experiences Attributes/culture
Organizational/structural capital (OC/SC)	Contracts Intellectual property/copyrights Digitized collections Access view policies Quality and safety assurance/certifications Branding Knowledge-based teams Learning culture Information about the staff Remote information services Systems for accessing databases Systems for network development User surveys
Relational capital (RC)	User relationship Networking and cooperation among libraries Participation in innovation networks Personnel networks Cooperation Trust/loyalty User training

provides some examples of typical library intangible assets categorized into human, organizational/structural, and relational.

Kostagiolas and Asonitis (2009) have discussed the practical and theoretical significance of intangible asset management within academic libraries, and have analyzed intellectual capital issues concerning all types of libraries. The authors also discussed the significance of some indicative intangible assets. Using the same classification—that is, human, organizational (or structural), and relational capital—they studied staff training, team development, experience, flexibility as regards human capital and library automation, innovation, patents, and management systems (business plans, quality certification) in respect of organizational capital. Finally, regarding the relational capital category, Kostagiolas and Asonitis (2009) examined intellectual capital assets such as user lists, user training, and the participation in information networks. In a more recent work, Asonitis and Kostagiolas (2010) proposed a methodological framework, based on the Analytic Hierarchy Process (AHP) method, discussed later on, for establishing a hierarchy among the three main categories of intellectual capital (human, organizational, and relational) in libraries. The criterion applied to this hierarchy is the actual contribution of each of the intellectual capital categories to improving the library's performance. This hierarchy results from a calculation of the corresponding weights of each of the intellectual capital categories. A case study, implementing this framework, was conducted for Greek central public libraries. Although the literature directly related to library intangible assets is not extensive, a significant amount of work with indirect references to intellectual capital may deserve further mention. This extensive literature is indirectly related to the issue in the sense that the terms "intangible asset/knowledge asset" or "intellectual capital" may not be directly mentioned at all, even in cases where quite interesting research on specific intangibles is being presented. This large amount of loosely interconnected research could benefit from further analysis, so as to reveal the actual underlying importance of specific intangible assets within libraries.

Intangible assets, however, should not be viewed separately from tangible assets—that is, traditional library resources. Library intellectual capital should be examined in connection with current practices and other tangible assets. Andriessen (2004), for example, states that innovation plays a significant role in improving services and creates intellectual capital when combined with "traditional" resources. Innovative information technologies and the Internet provide an opportunity for incorporating intangible resources into traditional library resources, such as printed material, different registers and records. For instance, Web 2.0 services, such as a blog or an RSS or a forum, may support a user discussion for the printed library material and thus further develop the relational capital of a library. In fact, the adoption of clear and effective policies related to the identification, development, and evaluation of intellectual capital, as well as the study of intangible resources and the impact of the investments made in them, is essential in order to attain the library's economic goals and meet user requirements. A survey conducted by Broady-Preston and Felice (2006) in 2003/04 on the relations between the academic library of the University of Malta and its users reaches the conclusion that a library can regain the interest of its users by actions such as improving its technological infrastructure, staff and user training (students and academics), enriching its collection, and promoting the cooperation of academics and specialists. The majority of these actions (staff training, enriching the information value of the library's collection, training the customers and promoting cooperation) require investments in all intangible asset categories, namely human, organizational (or structural), and relational capital.

Defining intellectual capital management in libraries

Roos et al. (2005) provide a useful definition of intellectual capital management:

> Intellectual capital management is the deployment and management of intellectual capital resources and their transformation (into intellectual capital resources or traditional capital resources) to maximize the present value of the organization's value creation in the eyes of its stakeholders.

Investments in intellectual capital assets, such as those discussed in the previous paragraph, provide the library with an added value, which is shared among its stakeholders, increasing the overall library contribution to the community. Hence, the library's management team should regard intangibles as critical assets/resources that need to be identified, measured, and eventually financially valuated. Generally speaking, an increase in the amount of intangible resources within a library will diversify library outputs and strengthen the library against competition. Although the contribution of the intellectual capital in value creation within libraries is rather obvious, the intellectual capital management is based on the fact that a library's real value is not the one presented in the balance sheet of assets and liabilities. Actually, a library's total value is expressed as the sum of its financial position as presented in the balance sheet, along with the value of its intellectual capital.

Proper management actions and activities related to intangible assets are important for developing innovative library services based on the information behavior and needs of the users through the employment of specific online systems and databases, library acquisition practices, electronic document delivery systems, cooperation, etc. It is highly probable that the existence and development of intellectual capital assets increase the total value of the assets reported on the balance sheet of a library. There is an absence of a single commonly accepted framework for the identification and measurement of library intangible assets. One way to move forward would be to adopt the methodological approach proposed by the MERITUM[2] project for companies or organizations that have not begun to identify and measure their intangible assets, or are at the beginning of this process. This approach requires those working in the library (Figure 1.2):

1. initially to identify their intellectual capital assets/ resources and intangible investments;

2. to determine specific indices for the measurement and dissemination of the information related to them (Gallego and Rodríguez, 2005);

3. to monitor the effects of intangible investments on the development of intangible assets/resources and then to assume action for the mobilization of intangible resources aiming at value creation.

This action can then create new intangible assets or reject old ones, thus requiring a repetition of the abovementioned process. Therefore, the framework conducts measurements

| Figure 1.2 | Stages for the development of an intangible asset management system |

```
              ┌──────────────────┐
              │   Measurement    │
              └──────────────────┘
             ↗                    ↖
┌──────────────────┐      ┌──────────────────┐
│  Identification  │ ←──→ │     Action       │
└──────────────────┘      └──────────────────┘
```

Source: Sánchez et al., 2001.

using indices linked to intangible assets and the library's strategic goals. Hence, it is actually a scorecard-type method with the intangible assets being categorized into human capital, information/technology capital, and organizational capital. For instance, an intangible asset that can be classified under "human capital" is the actual quality of the library's staff (staff quality is determined by their ability to recruit new users/customers and maintain them over time, work in teams, be motivated by the goals that the library's management has set, and generally be flexible and comfortable with change). Intangibles classified under "structural capital" include library systems, databases and the level of IT literacy. Organizational capital includes the library's management, the existence of flexible service practices, the mobilization of available resources in order to achieve strategic goals, and the general culture of the library.

The overall library management strategy is presented in Figure 1.3 and includes actions for both tangible and intangible assets (left part of the figure), associated with intangible assets/resources (distinguished into the three intangible asset categories in the middle part of the figure). The right part of Figure 1.3 presents a set of indicators that may be used to measure the performance of the library and

Figure 1.3 Library intangible asset management framework

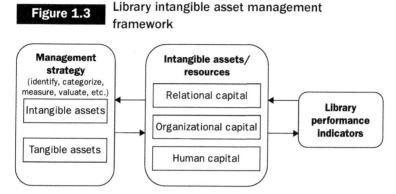

Source: Kostagiolas and Asonitis (2010).

thus provide guidance for management issues. Roos et al. (2005) suggest that the library's management team should make judgments based on the following three aspects of intellectual capital resources:

1. How influential is a given intangible resource upon the organization's ability to create value?

2. What is the level of quality held by the intangible asset as compared to the ideal intangible asset quality?

3. How many intangible resources should the organization acquire, compared to an ideal situation?

The identification and evaluation of intellectual capital, along with the above mentioned issues, constitute a rather challenging environment for the management of intellectual capital in libraries and information services.

It is rather obvious, however, that not all intellectual capital resources hold the same importance within the library's process of value creation. A first step towards managing intellectual capital would be to identify the intangible assets that have the highest positive effect on library stakeholder viewpoints. For instance, the main concern of a corporate library is to maximize the company's financial returns. This, however, might not be the case for non-profit libraries, such as academic and/or public libraries. Vasconcelos (2008) recommended focusing on the unique features of each organization or enterprise, where most of its value lies. Roos et al. (2005) set five requirements for the utilization of intangible assets, which are:

1. to be valuable, in the sense that they are able to support the library's strategic goals;

2. to be durable, in the sense that they preserve their attributes over time;

3. to be scarce, in the sense that they are not easily accessible by potential competitors;

4. to be inimitable, in the sense that a potential imitator will experience significant costs for their duplication;

5. to be irreplaceable, in the sense that a substitute is difficult, if not impossible, to develop.

A similar effort to develop a general framework for recording intangible resources and assessing their value (framework for the valuation of intangible assets) was undertaken by Andreou et al. (2007) and was based on the eight value drivers as defined by Green and Ryan (2005): customers, competitors, employees, information, partners, processes, products/services, and technology. These drivers were linked to four specific administrative goals (innovation, organization, socialization, and culture) in order to identify and manage intangible assets. The identification and the subsequent recording of intangible assets were based on two parameters: the added value generated by each intangible asset and the critical indicators of success/ performance (CSF, Critical Success Factors) related to the useful life of each intangible asset. The value of a library is a complex combination of the economic, cultural, social, and intellectual contribution to those who directly use its services or indirectly obtain benefits from the existence of the library itself and the services it provides (British Library, 2004).

Subsequent to their identification and categorization, the valuation of an intangible asset may be necessary for determining, for instance, their price of sale, use, supply or concession or, in a supplementary way, takeovers or mergers, tax treatment, or assistance in several legal proceedings (Reilly and Schweihs, 1998). Intangible asset financial valuation methods that are presented in Chapter 5 are distinguished into three categories (Reilly and Schweihs, 1998): the cost approach, the market approach, and the income approach. The cost approach depends upon the analytical methods of reproduction, replacement, creation, cost aversion, historical prices, etc., and on the concept of intangible asset substitutes. The market approach, on the other hand, includes valuation methods that are based on the analysis of assets that are similar to the intangible asset under valuation, known as comparables, for which recent transaction data are available (e.g. sales or concessions of license of use). The income approach includes the analytical valuation processes that are based on the discounting of future income that is expected to occur due to the use or possession of the intangible asset under valuation. Despite the fact that there have been some very important efforts, such as those mentioned above and those carried out through certain inter-sector researches (e.g. Gallego and Rodríguez, 2005) there are no library-specific studies on intangible asset valuation.

In order to evaluate the intellectual capital of an organization, Vasconcelos et al. (2001) proposed the so-called "relationship to product versus content dilemma." They expressed the uncertainty that characterizes any estimation or measurement of the intellectual capital. Frequently, the value of the intangible asset depends upon the context of its deployment and it often "lies in the eye of the beholder" (Vasconcelos, 2008). The author also suggested that one should focus on a specific time or on the library's future, based on its strategic goals. A library's value can be expressed as a financial value (in monetary terms) or as a numerical measurement of the library's total contribution to the economy, calculated using a set of indicators that measure knowledge-based services (e.g. Missingham, 2005). The latter is based on the concept of ROI (return on investment) and the contingent valuation method (Missingham, 2005). ROI measures the net benefit/loss generated by a monetary unit invested in a company/organization and is calculated as the percentage of the ratio between the net profit/loss and the relative amount of the investment (Kannan and Aulbur, 2004). The contingent valuation method (Missingham, 2005) is a quantitative economic methodology, supported by a panel of scientists including Nobel Prize winners Kenneth Arrow and Robert Solow, which estimates the total benefit of a non-market good derived from publicly funded organizations or programs. The contingent valuation method is based on the estimation of the amount of money an individual would be prepared to pay in order to maintain access to the underlying good. Missingham (2005) supports the notion that the set of indicators, developed by the Australian Bureau of Statistics, related to innovation and entrepreneurship, human capital, and information and communication technology (ICT), can be used to assess a library's contribution to the knowledge economy.

Over the past decades, the competition among libraries has become all the more intense, mainly due to the existence of Internet services that are in competition with the services traditionally provided by libraries. For example, "Google

Scholar" is a free search engine specializing in academic publications. Therefore, the members of the academic community could use "Google Scholar" as a starting point for scholarly searches rather than their academic library. On the other hand, publishers often have contractual agreements with institutions (for example, universities) and/or networks of libraries. Hence, individual libraries function as the proxy for the agreement between the publisher and the institution or network. In this case, free information, shared through the Internet, is considered to be a service competing with the ones provided by libraries. Google's ambitious "Google Books Library Project" may also evolve to be a service in competition with those provided by public libraries. According to Google (2010), the aim of this project is to:

> ... make it easier for people to find relevant books—specifically, books they wouldn't find any other way such as those that are out of print—while carefully respecting authors' and publishers' copyrights. Our ultimate goal is to work with publishers and libraries to create a comprehensive, searchable, virtual card catalog of all books in all languages that helps users discover new books and publishers discover new readers.

To survive in the long run, libraries need to manage and thus utilize intellectual capital resources.

The overall aim is to make good use of intellectual capital assets. Small-scale investments in library intangible assets (as compared to those made in tangible assets) may yield benefits way beyond the invested capital. Motivating library management teams to participate in professional networks is an example of such action. The participation of libraries in collaborative networks adds significantly to the intellectual capital of the library by:

- enabling broader access to the available information material (e.g. databases, documents);

- improving human capital (e.g. skills, competencies, experience, and teamwork);

- sharing experiences or actions aiming at structural capital assets (e.g. management techniques and practices, user surveys, software platforms access for heterogeneous data storage, and retrieval environments); and

- improving relational capital (e.g. relationship marketing, trust development, user training programs in information literacy and lifelong learning).

All these actions can lead to the development of innovative information services that are difficult for competitors to imitate. Invisible and unsurpassed quality along with the provision of an integrated system of components that serve differentiated needs is also difficult to imitate. Whatever their type, libraries can accumulate clear-cut benefits from providing services that are hard, or almost impossible, to imitate and have lower prices, have a longer useful remaining life expectancy, and offer sustainable cash flow (benefits).

Summary

Libraries do not remain unaffected by their ever-changing environment and for a number of analysts, reductions in funding are now a harsh reality for certain libraries while others face similar problems. A significant number of issues related to the management of intellectual capital in libraries have been identified, along with the role that libraries play within a new knowledge-based economic environment. Andriessen (2004) points out that market globalization combined with the reduction of international transaction barriers (for example, to goods and services, and investments) and the growth of ICT are key drivers for the new economy. If this is true, libraries and information services potentially have a significant role to play within this new financial environment. Libraries can distribute, through their services and systems, a core segment of all necessary knowledge and information required by the current global competitive economic environment. On the other hand, libraries all over the world face the pressure of competition and are urged to modernize their management procedures and other systems.

Like any innovative concept, intellectual capital has created dilemmas, since we can only approximate the degree to which we gain advantage from an intellectual capital management activity. The extent and expansion of this threat, however, may push libraries to take immediate action. In addition, increased competition and pressure from global economic threats may also force libraries to act immediately. Managing intangibles allows the library's administration to identify its core intangible assets and evaluate the effectiveness of the investments made in them. The results of intellectual capital management should be presented and used complementarily to annual financial reports. This would provide library stakeholders with all the necessary information in order to keep track of all the steps taken so that the library can assume a prominent role within future economic and social realities. Managing distinct categories of intellectual capital may require different approaches based on conceptual frameworks from different disciplines. For instance, one may use market criteria to evaluate a library's relational capital, but this is not the case for human capital. This would involve a disciplinary shift, from an accounting model to a non-accounting one. The resolution of different viewpoints for the management of intellectual capital cannot take place within the conceptual framework of a single discipline.

Notes

1. *www.reference.com/browse/intellectual+capital*
2. The MERITUM (MEasuRing Intangibles To Understand and improve innovation Management) project is being funded by the TSER project (Targeted Socio-Economic Research) of the European Union. Several European universities and organizations have taken part in this project (Spain (coordinator), France, Finland, Sweden, Denmark, and Norway) (Cañibano et al., 1999). The project actions began in November 1998 and were completed by April 2001 (Sánchez et al., 2001).

2

Libraries' Worlds of Production and intellectual capital utilization

Abstract: Chapter 1 introduced the fundamental concepts and issues of library intellectual capital. Furthermore, the level of libraries' intellectual capital management awareness is being linked to their survival within a competitive economic environment, where the core product is knowledge itself. On the other hand, the development of this intellectual capital consciousness may promote libraries as key organizations for the creation of a valuable network of information and knowledge creators/distributors. In this chapter, the utilization of intangible assets is explored by analyzing their role within the framework proposed by Stopper and Salais (1997) for the analysis of different economic models, referred to as the Worlds of Production. This framework includes four Worlds of Production: industrial, market, interpersonal, and intellectual. Each "World" is a conventional socioeconomic construct, appearing as a set of rules and norms, coordination and operation practices among organizations and enterprises that develop specific information services.

Key words: intellectual capital utilization, Worlds of Production, industrial world, market world, interpersonal world, intellectual world.

The worlds of intellectual capital utilization

Intellectual capital assets have been part of human activities ever since the origins of our civilization (Baruch, 2001; Lev, 2001). Although one may safely assume that some intangible assets were somehow always present within human economies (for example, the experience and competences of the workforce), their conscious utilization within the production process has only been observed during the past few decades. In fact, as Hand and Lev (2003) point out, in the United States of America, investments in intangible assets, including Research and Development (R&D) and software development, have impressively increased over the past 20 years. As opposed to intangible assets, investments in tangible assets (such as plant facilities and equipment) during the 1990s remain largely unchanged as compared to those made during the 1950s and 1960s. The shift towards investments in intellectual capital can be attributed to the unprecedented advances of ICTs, the Internet, and the fearsome competition caused by market globalization. In the modern era, value is not only associated with the allocation of capital or tangible assets, but also with innovation and knowledge, which seem to be the main wealth-producing resources (Andriessen, 2004).

The existing intense competition calls for the utilization of intellectual capital, accumulating it through a cooperation of distinct organizations as well as users, suppliers, or even competitors. This competition also promotes creativity and innovation, through the utilization of human resources and new management techniques. Globalization and the advances in information technologies are the main causes of an enormous increase in the utilization of intangible assets over the past decades. Beginning in the mid-1970s, the current globalization process was supported by the status quo of three worldwide dominant currencies (dollar, euro, and yen) and the liberation of capital circulation (OECD, 2005). Libraries in both their tangible forms (for example, infrastructure, equipment, and traditional collections) and their intangible forms (for example, digital collections, automation systems, and networking synergies) are becoming very important for businesses and enterprises. Harris (2002) recognizes that within this process of globalization the development of innovation, entrepreneurship, and synergies among employees, customers, suppliers, or even competitors, the utilization of physical and human resources, as well as innovative marketing strategies, are considered to be essential. With the exception of physical resources, all other factors identified by Harris (2002) are intangible in nature. Libraries have the opportunity, if not the responsibility, to participate actively in the establishment of a new economic reality that relies heavily upon information and knowledge. It is an undisputed fact that within the new intellectual economy, driven by ICTs, libraries can actually coach the business community, which is currently in a discovery process, by using well-established library practices (Kostagiolas and Bohoris, 2010).

Intellectual capital has been historically related to libraries, in terms of their services, administration, and culture. Libraries traditionally use and/or produce intellectual assets. Koenig (1997) characteristically stated that a librarian's first response to the management of intellectual capital is likely to be: "Hold on. We have been in the knowledge management business, the intellectual capital business for years. What do these people think a library is, anyway?" In this chapter, the framework of Stopper and Salais (1997) based on the four Worlds of Production (industrial, market, interpersonal, and intellectual) is employed for analyzing the utilization of intellectual capital investments over the years (Kostagiolas and Asonitis, 2009). The Worlds of Production framework is employed for studying intangible asset utilization in library production models. The analysis includes all three intangible asset categories: human, structural, and relational capital.

The "Worlds of Production" framework analyzed for libraries

As stated before, the main aim of this chapter is to examine the use of intangible assets in the light of the diversity and complexity of the ever-changing library environment. Before proceeding any further, it might be useful to present briefly the Worlds of Production framework, as introduced by Stopper and Salais (1997). The Worlds of Production can be seen as a theoretical discussion method for classifying new realities and proposing an analytical framework that explicitly tackles changes in the economy. Stopper and Salais (1997) introduced the four "Worlds of Production" in an effort to categorize different eras in the economy. In that sense, each "World of Production" comprises a distinct and complete framework, not necessarily in time order, within which specific rules, conventions, organizational logic, and requirements are being developed. According to the terminology used to describe the Worlds of Production as presented by Stopper and Salais (1997), the different categories are: the Industrial World, the Market World, the Interpersonal World, and the World of Intellectual Resources. Within the Industrial World framework, products and services are examined on the basis of the relations created between stakeholders. Therefore, products and services are categorized under the four Worlds of Production based on whom they are produced for and not according to their material substance, conventional or digital.

The Industrial Library World for libraries includes the following characteristics.

1. Library services are impersonal, substitutable, generic, and serve undifferentiated needs of specific groups of scholars.

2. Libraries compete in the field of physical status improvements and collection richness.

3. Library operations and services are based solely on tangible material objects (printed collections, conventional cataloging methods, etc.).

4. The library's printed material is substitutable, which means that the various items can be replaced or transferred from one person or place to another, while library collections have no individual character.

5. Library operations and services are static in the sense that the librarian's contribution has very small impact on stable bureaucratic organizational structures.

The Market Library World includes libraries with the following characteristics.

1. Library building location and status are important and library operations and services are hybrid, that is, they encompass printed and electronic material mainly originating from the physical and administrative bounds of the library.

2. Library operations and services are targeted towards specific market segments.

3. Standards and guidelines for organizing library collections are operationally incorporated.

4. Libraries compete in the fields of production cost and direct response to demand, while organizational innovations are encouraged in order to reduce the time

required to handle large collections and respond to user demand.

5. Libraries build networks for conventional collection, experience, and technology sharing (for example, interlibrary loan services).

The Interpersonal Library World includes libraries with the following characteristics.

1. Library operations and services are hybrid or digital, so they encompass conventional and digital material within and outside of the library's physical and administrative bounds.

2. Libraries become personalized and are designed to satisfy specific needs of particular communities widely dispersed throughout the network.

3. Library operations are extended in order to incorporate new and traditional material, regardless of its form or format.

4. Location is not that important within an Impersonal World industry, since library services are based on both electronic material and interlibrary networks developed for conventional library material.

5. Formal relations based upon direct mutual understanding are established among stakeholders who share knowledge based on long-lasting relations and content-rich transactions for information interchange over wide information networks.

The World of Intellectual Library Resources has the following characteristics.

1. Library services include intellectual activities that aim to improve the quality of the existing user actions in their work-lines and their life-lines, or create new ones.

2. The knowledge produced through this intellectual activity is linked to theories, concepts, and formal technological and management methods.

3. Investments are related to innovation, quality, and R&D.

4. Library professionals assume roles with wider impact and develop generally applicable new knowledge, such as protocols, practices, and rules, thus gaining ongoing intellectual knowhow from their career.

5. Relations with other actors largely depend on confidence and trust, and new methods of communication and promotion, such as library blogs and book blogs.

The discussion presented above includes a wide range of library types ranging from conventional libraries to hybrid and digital libraries. Libraries have come a long way over the years, moving from an industrial production framework to the intellectual World of Production era of the new millennium. Now there are thousands of libraries of all types worldwide and they have all managed to adjust to new socioeconomic realities. Amazingly enough, libraries include and will include the memory and the future of civilization as we know it. The current financial depression and rapid technological changes require the utilization of libraries' intellectual content and potential contributions to all aspects of economy and society, so that we may enjoy libraries for many centuries to come. The Worlds of Production library taxonomy expands and extends the traditional library through the integration of innovative information technologies, new processes, and media. It should further be noted, however, that the Worlds of Production framework goes beyond the "historical" (chronological) taxonomy, which means that nowadays all the worlds can coexist, expressing different variables around the world. Thus, the industrial world can be found in a small conventional library in a rural area or an underdeveloped school library. The market and interpersonal worlds may express the vast majority of libraries of all types (public, academic, hospital, etc.). The intellectual world expresses the transition to the next library generation of Web 2.0, for example, the Public Library 2.0 (Chowdhury et al., 2006), based on a social, mobile, and open organizational culture and service orientation that can be found in prominent libraries worldwide (the Library of Congress, the British Library, and the Library of Alexandria, among others).

Moreover, for each of the distinct Worlds of Production, a unique model of production has been introduced by the authors. A model of production can be defined as "the set of routines, organizational structures and operational principles which guide the firm from day to day and year to year" (Stopper and Salais, 1997). In the Industrial Production model, library services change over time, requiring fixed investments, especially in tangible assets, which can assure low production costs under a rather steady competition environment. In the Market Production model, production focuses on specific segments of the market (specific population groups and/or specific groups of scholars). Production is still conventional but competition is conditioned by demand satisfaction. The Interpersonal Production model is characterized by a diversification in library service quality and quantity within a family of services that satisfy similar purposes. Organizational flexibility, personalized relationships with the users, and the use of specialized information technology and the Internet are the requirements for a successful activity within the interpersonal model. Economies of variety are being developed in this world. Finally, in the Intellectual Production model, production is based on innovative services and the use of specialized information technologies, investments in Research and Development

(R&D), highly educated, experienced, and specialized professional teams, and flexible organizational structures.

The same library may include all four Worlds of Production in its development through time. Historical libraries that continue to play an important role have for the most part exploited the opportunities of all four worlds. The Biblioteca Marciana (National Library of St. Mark's) in Venice is a typical example. Founded in 1537—after the donation of Cardinal Bessarion's famous collection to Venice in 1476—it was the library of a city and not of a nobleman or a monastery. The role and work of chief librarians, the famous building by architect J. Sansovino, collections of manuscripts and printed material, as well as legislation and decisions taken by those in political power, led to the development of the library throughout its first phase (industrial). Famous since its foundation, the Marciana Library passed through all three other Worlds of Production. Efforts were made for a more rational organization of the library, and collaboration with scientists, scholars, politicians, and artists took place. New methods for storing and retrieving information and providing access to books had been applied and new methods had been introduced as regards reader needs and expectations. It must be noted that chief librarians in the Renaissance and the Enlightenment were usually scholars of noble descent. They were men of letters and men of political power at the same time. A few of them went on to become Doges later on.

As libraries evolved, moving from one production world to another, they differentiated their operations and their services in terms of material circulation (for example, handling of user accounts, loaning, returning, and shelving), reference and other information services (for example, answering user questions, gaining access to specific reference material), collection maintenance (for example, cataloging materials, classification, preservation), collection development (for example, ordering materials and subscriptions budgets), and information technology (for example, developing and maintaining databases, web services). During the Enlightenment and the Industrial Revolution, the enlargement of the reading audience combined with social, political, financial, and cultural factors led to libraries being "free to all, open to all" (Lerner, 2001). With the dawn of each era, the diachronic aims and values of libraries matured and were enriched by the needs and demands of the reading audience along with economic, social, cultural, and economic factors. When A. Panizzi was appointed Keeper of Printed Books at the British Museum in 1837, he set forth an ambitious plan to satisfy the needs of the library and the expectations of the readers, taking into consideration economic, social, and cultural factors. Apart from the cataloging rules, he enriched the collection, securing a substantial appropriation from Parliament and building the secular reading room (Lerner, 2001).

Although the Worlds of Production have a chronological succession, occurring one after the other, it should be noted that within each World of Production one can find features pertaining to previous models. Figure 2.1 indicates that earlier models of production may be present in successful Worlds of Production. For instance, the Industrial, Market, and Interpersonal Models of production are clearly present in the Interpersonal World of Production. Therefore, a specific library may be able to adopt the model of production that best serves its interests within the current Intellectual Resources World. If further studied, the above-mentioned suggestion may provide an industry-specific analysis for choosing the best-suited organizational approach, according to each different World of Production. Intellectual capital assets exist in all four Worlds of Production, but the rate of their utilization varies significantly.

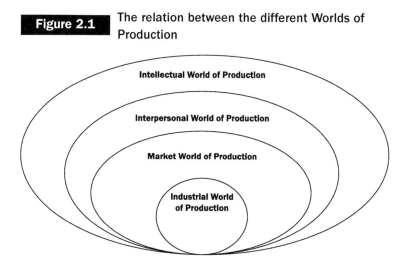

Figure 2.1 The relation between the different Worlds of Production

Libraries' intangible resources utilization within the Worlds of Production framework

Intellectual capital assets belonging to all categories (human capital, structural capital, and intellectual capital) were diachronically present in the economy and in any production model and/or World of Production. However, the way they were perceived and utilized varies significantly. Table 2.1 provides an analysis of the utilization of intangible assets for each of the four Worlds of Production (Industrial, Market, Interpersonal, and Intellectual). In order to comment on the use of intangible assets within the different Worlds of Production, a threefold methodology needs to be adopted. Firstly, a horizontal analysis of the information provided in Table 2.1 may enable changes to be identified in the utilization of a specific type of intangibles over time. For example, human capital is largely ignored in the Industrial World, while it becomes increasingly significant from the Market

Table 2.1 Utilization of intangibles in the Worlds of Production

Intangible categories	Worlds of Production			
	Industrial	Market	Interpersonal	Intellectual
HC	Practical skills and experience in library practices	Experience, specialized skills, and training	Experience, specialized skills, training, and flexibility	Knowledge, experience, innovation and creativity, and flexibility
SC	Library operation and service provision know-how Library's conventional material	Library operation and service provision knowhow adjusted to different market segments Actions to reduce the time required for responding to demand Library's mainly conventional material	Flexibility (to adjust library services to customer demand) Highly automated and specialized library operations Library's conventional and digital material and services for extensive market territories Special routines to communicate information to users	Flexibility (a culture for personalized operations and services) Services and operations based on highly specialized staff competences Digital strategy in cooperation with other memory institutions (specialized library services to serve more extensive market territories and specific market segments)

RC	Relations between libraries and patrons	Relations among libraries and between libraries and networks of external information suppliers (e.g. publishers)	Personalized relationships based on direct mutual understanding with the users and other organizations, suppliers, and enterprises	Relations based on confidence and mutual respect towards common aims in win-win understanding
Intangible assets utilization	**Low utilization**	**Small to moderate utilization**	**Moderate to high utilization**	**High to extensive utilization**
	Investments in intangibles mostly relate to the structural capital for improving library operations	Investments in intangibles mostly relate to organizational innovations and less to relations within networks Human capital is playing an important role and trained library personnel are required	Investments in intangibles for managing relations within library networks and with other information providers, and publishers for satisfying user requirements Organizational structure is becoming more flexible Human capital is becoming quite important, and highly trained staff are required	Investments in intangibles are related to the economy of knowledge, which is based, among others, on innovative ICTs and the Internet Library processes are simplified and reorganized, promoting flexibility Human capital is very important and the personnel consists of highly specialized library professionals

Source: Adapted from Kostagiolas and Asonitis (2008).

and the Interpersonal World onwards to the Intellectual World. Secondly, a vertical analysis can be applied to each specific World of Production in order to examine the utilization of intangibles in a holistic way. The third approach focuses on libraries and examines the utilization of intangible assets, using a combination of the production models found in all Worlds of Production.

An analysis of human capital utilization within all Worlds of Production is provided in the first row of Table 2.1. There is no doubt that intangible assets, such as experience, specialized skills, knowledge, and flexibility, existed in libraries even during the Industrial World. However, they were not properly utilized and as Stopper and Salais (1997) point out, "the particular qualities of persons disappear, to be replaced by roles, tasks and positions within a hierarchy." In the Market World, the production is still serial and thus intangible assets embodied within human capital are scarcely utilized, although specialized skills are required for library operations, services, and other administrative and management tasks. In the Interpersonal World, quality-based competition requires a significant number of workers with specialized skills in production and a relatively higher utilization of human capital. Library professionals in the Interpersonal World implement a practical knowhow in order to create quality products and services. A complete utilization of human capital is only required in the Intellectual Library World of Production. The creation of new knowledge and innovation is quite significant for the economy and society, turning labor into the main productivity factor, while other intangibles such as knowledge, experience, creativity, and flexibility are also being used.

Specific library organizational practices and production tools are intangible assets embodied in the structural capital, and can be identified in all four Worlds of Production, as shown in Table 2.1. However, bureaucratic library organization hierarchies, although heavily criticized, have been considered to offer a more propitious environment for innovation than the flexible, "post-bureaucratic" organizational structures (Harris, 2006). Other intangible assets embodied within structural capital (computer software, databases, patents, and copyrights) are more extensively utilized when library services need to be of personalized nature, e.g. in the Intellectual World, with their use declining as we move from the Interpersonal World on to the Market and Industrial Worlds. An example of the declining use of structural capital as we move backwards from the Intellectual to the Industrial World is the digital library material (in the Intellectual World) as opposed to a traditional library with only conventional printed material (in the Interpersonal World). While digital libraries operate mainly through acquiring copyrights from content handlers, a conventional library has probably no copyrights in its possession.

The change in use of relational capital from the Industrial to the Intellectual World of Production can be examined through a horizontal approach based on the information provided in Table 2.1. Relational capital in the Market and Interpersonal Worlds is expressed through the relations among libraries and between libraries and networks of external information suppliers and publishers. The main aim of those relations and subscriptions is to enrich the library's information content. In the Interpersonal World the relational capital is used more extensively as compared to the two previously mentioned Worlds. Relational capital does not exist just in signing contracts with suppliers and publishers but mostly in creating personal relations between the library and each individual user. Relations in the Interpersonal World are based on mutual understanding between the producer-firm and the customer (Stopper and Salais, 1997). These relations may or may not be formal (e.g. user subscriptions) but are being confirmed and developed in day-to-day practice between the two parts. In the Intellectual World, relational capital is being extensively utilized. We can identify intangibles deriving from contracts, the relationships between the library and its users, or between the librarians and the users. Relations in the Intellectual World are based on confidence, trust, and mutual respect. In the Intellectual World, when a library professional comes to (or leaves) a library they bring (or take) with them not only a part of the firm's human capital value but also a part of the firm's relational capital, since relations in the Intellectual World are not absolutely vested in the library itself (contracts, relationships between the firm and its customers), but also depend upon each individual person (Kostagiolas and Asonitis, 2009).

For libraries there might be cases where a market or even an industrial production model may be sufficient. For example, in a conventional school library serving a rather small community, the administration might focus mainly on investments in human capital and less on structural and relational capital. On the other hand, an academic library requires the most up-to-date intellectual model of production, which should be based heavily on intangible asset investments of all three types. The library's relations with its stakeholders, customers, potential customers, suppliers, and partners are valuable intangible assets (White, 2007A), embodied in its relational capital. Library relational capital, as a sustainability factor, is perhaps more important for academic libraries than for any other library type. The information needs of the community that libraries serve are growing rapidly, forcing them to participate in information networks set up by other academic libraries, publishers, electronic journals, information services, etc., instead of trying to expand their own collection (Sheng and Sun, 2007).

The analysis of intangible asset utilization, as provided in this chapter, attempts to explore and highlight the fact that an effective exploitation of intangible assets, combined with innovation and information, should form an integral part of the management operations and activities within every library. However, we should avoid generalizations since a single World of Production model cannot be appropriate for all types of libraries. This may be justified by the fact that libraries are rather unique organizations, being throughout their long history both tangible and intangible in nature. For a library, fixed investments in real assets and particularly in buildings are absolutely essential. Tangible investments in furniture (e.g. workstations, seats, and study carrels) and office equipment (e.g. photocopiers) are necessary for every library. Childs (2006) provides a number of examples illustrating that tangible investments in refurbishment, location, and new building projects are an effective way to attract new library users. Investments in intangible assets may include the recruitment of specialized personnel, small-scale training programs, and acquiring special software to support library services. In other cases, however, library operations demand substantial investments in any of the three intellectual capital categories: human, organizational (structural), and relational. Such cases include, for example, digital libraries and/or research/academic libraries (Kostagiolas and Asonitis, 2009), where the library staff quality, team development, copyrights, computer software and databases, participation in information networks, etc., are absolutely essential.

Summary

In this chapter, the Worlds of Production framework for libraries was employed in order to study and understand the utilization of library intellectual capital according to different economic/production models. This theoretical analysis examines the utilization of intellectual capital within the different socioeconomic models presented in the Worlds of Production framework. It is certain that the existence or the creation of intangible assets increases the value of the services/products provided and improves their efficiency, effectiveness, and quality. Nowadays, different production models may actually coexist and it is not necessary for all libraries, whether older or newly founded ones, to follow strictly the modern approach of the Intellectual World of Production. On the contrary, libraries might be able to acquire certain features from previous Worlds of Production, utilizing tangible and intangible assets according to the existing socioeconomic context.

3

Identifying and categorizing intellectual capital in libraries

Abstract: Chapter 1 attempted to define intellectual capital, analyze different types of intellectual capital resources, and examine the content and significance of intellectual capital management. Furthermore, the significance of identifying and managing intellectual capital assets for libraries has been discussed as compared to traditional economic resources (monetary and physical). In Chapter 2, the innovative framework of Stopper and Salais (1997) was employed for analyzing the use of intangible assets in libraries categorized into different Worlds of Production of different orientation as regards their operations and services. Due to the economic pressure and fierce competition, library stakeholders are expecting that their library's administration should increase library value by exploiting significant intangible assets. In this chapter, we will further explore methods for identifying and understanding the potential of library intangible assets. This is a fundamental step in the intellectual capital management process.

Key words: intellectual property, copyrights, open access, contracts, goodwill, competition, cooperation, co-opetition.

The need to identify and understand specific intangible assets

The categorization of the Worlds of Production, as well as the analysis that will take place in this chapter as regards intellectual capital asset identification, provides a background of information, requirements, and characteristics for intangible asset management. Before proceeding, however, it might be useful to clarify further the differences between tangible and intangible resources. As we have seen, intellectual capital resources, similar to conventional economic resources, which include monetary and physical, are divided into three categories: relational, organizational, and human. Tangible assets have a physical existence and substantial form, and may be mobile or immobile. This distinction, however, is not sufficient since some intangible assets such as a contract, a copyright registration, a pattern registration, or a user list, have a physical presence as well. A distinction between tangible and intangible assets is provided in a simple and clear way by Reilly and Schweihs (1998).

- The value of a tangible asset/resource is created by its tangible nature.

- The value of an intangible asset/resource is created by its intangible nature.

Libraries are unique organizations, managing resources that are both tangible and intangible in nature. Furthermore, in some cases tangible resources are associated with intangible resources or are integrated into them. The printed book collection, for example, is both tangible and intangible in nature. The value of the books as tangible assets is resulting from library property rights associated with the book as a commercial product, but at the same time there is a value associated with the use of the book's content as an intangible resource serving library users. In a similar manner, one may argue that a tangible asset (e.g. a computer) is actually required for managing the intangible library information system of collection circulation. The same party (the library) may have the rights to use an intangible asset, but may or may not own the tangible assets required to explore its value. For instance, a library may have access to information material but may not possess the proper infrastructure for using it. In fact, within the library setting, intellectual capital assets significantly enhance the value of the tangible assets that are associated with their utilization and vice versa. On the other hand, intangible assets may be viewed distinctly and separately from any tangible asset. In other cases, a library that intends to profit from the value of a particular intangible asset may or may not possess the associated tangible assets or may possess only a part of the tangible assets required, being, for example, within an information network and sharing resources with others.

Many authors wanting to venture into the identification and definition of intellectual capital (or intangible assets) in a managerial perspective (rather than an economic, accountant, or taxation perspective) employed the concept of "resource" rather than the concept of "asset," with a view to overcome issues associated with property and ownership. A very interesting analysis of the relationship between intangible assets and property (or ownership) is provided by Reilly and Schweihs (1998). For the rest of this book, the term "resources" is preferred, although it is used interchangeably with the term "assets." Roos et al. (2005) defined four criteria for identifying intellectual capital resources, based on the categorization of Figure 3.1:

1. completeness (each intangible asset must be distinctly identified and defined separately from of all other library resources);

2. distinctness (each intangible asset must be complete in a sense that no other relevant resource(s) is missing from a given category of the identification tree of Figure 3.1);

3. independence (each intangible asset must be independent from all other resources, in a way that if one of these resources changes in quality or quantity, there must be no automatic and immediate change in any of the other resources);

4. agreeability (the resource distinction tree of Figure 3.1 must be broken down and stakeholders should agree that it is suitable for the library's purposes).

Our aim is to put forward a management paradigm by extending and not rejecting those that already exist, namely

Figure 3.1 **Conventional and intellectual library resources identification method**

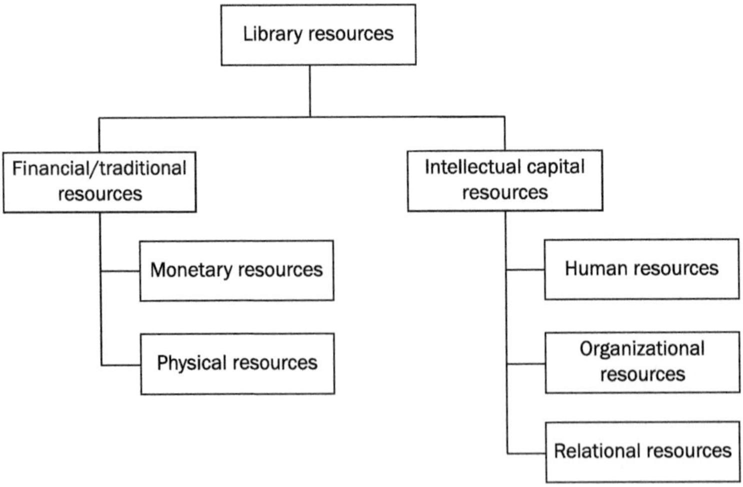

Source: Based on Roos et al. (2005).

the tangible asset economy and other common library management practices. This leads us to the belief that the creation and reinforcement of intangible assets must form part of any integral management strategy. We acknowledge, however, that highlighting the importance of intangible assets is only one part of the total research topic, which may include quantitative and qualitative analyses on the identification, measurement, valuation, reporting, and exploration of intangible assets in library management and economy, intangible asset lifecycles, etc. Figure 3.1 provides a general resource categorization method for libraries which includes financial assets such as equity, retained earnings, working capital, prepaid expenses, accounts receivables, etc. and physical assets such as land, machinery, inventory, plants, trucks, etc. In this perspective, every organization can be viewed as a collection of tangible and intangible resources that have been combined in a certain way in order to achieve certain aims (Ross et al., 2005). The objective of intellectual capital management is to ensure that value is maximized by exploiting both components of the available library resources.

Libraries face significant challenges when trying to identify their resources. In fact, libraries' tangible and intangible assets can be further analyzed within each of the categories of financial, physical, human, organizational (or structural), and relational resources. A detailed classification of intangible assets under these distinct categories is an important first step towards the creation of a library measurement, valuation, and reporting strategy. As we gradually approach library intangible assets or intellectual capital, one may feel that there is a change in our behaviors and expectations as regards investments and their effect on library operations and services, as well as other issues including quality and user satisfaction. An additional advantage is that the process of identifying tangible and intangible resources enhances the understanding not only of each individual resource but also of all resources that the organization has at its disposal and that have the potential to contribute to library value creation (Roos et al., 2005). In many cases, resources such as partnerships with other libraries and information suppliers or relations with specific user groups get overlooked. The following paragraphs will aim at identifying such issues. However, we should not disregard the fact that each library is unique as regards the combinations of its tangible and intangible resources.

An analysis of library intellectual capital resources

Some indicative examples of intellectual capital resources were listed in Figure 3.1 (page 52). This illustration, however, is not complete and has only an introductory role. A quite extensive illustrative listing of intangible assets, resources, and intellectual properties is provided by Mard et al. (2007). As mentioned before, each library should be considered as a unique organization and there is no straightforward way to provide rules for combinations of specific human, organizational, and relational capital resources that better serve its purposes. Intellectual capital resources, provided that the requirements of completeness, distinctness, independence, and agreeability are satisfied, can be identified in relation to the following three aspects:

1. the library's value and contribution towards the wider organization/system within which it operates, e.g. the hospital for a hospital library or the society as a whole for a public library;

2. legal rights and ownership status;

3. collection development and future value.

Library management needs to define the internal (staff, collection, infrastructure, etc.) and external (economics, politics, society, technology, etc.) dimensions of the library's environment, as well as historical or traditional aspects that affect value creation. Therefore, a public library on a small Greek island needs to utilize its intellectual capital resources in a different way than a public library near London or a non-profit research library in New York.

Based on the above-mentioned suggestion, the proposed theoretical framework for analyzing intellectual capital resources may be further specialized through research of specific intangible assets related to a specific library type or a particular library. Intellectual capital library management should aim at improving the current level of user options, or create new ones for titles or information resources. Intellectual capital management philosophy requires libraries to create value by "making everything available," digitizing their collections to make them both electronically and physically available, and providing a broad range of information beyond local holdings. New innovative services are being developed in order to help connect the library collection to its users and increase the number of user options. Relational capital attempts, among others, to incorporate information resources from other libraries and commercial publishers, so as to expand user options, provide familiar entry points and allow users to express their likes and dislikes. The library's staff may develop and introduce new practices of general nature, not specialized to a specific library operation or service.

Libraries are organizations that need to guarantee the provision of reliable and high-quality educational, cultural, entertainment, and government material to the public. One important aspect of this historical mission is the management of a library's intellectual property rights. Intellectual property rights are intangible asset generators but represent a portion of the overall intellectual capital of a modern library. The term "intellectual property" refers to the ownership by the copyright owners (e.g. creators), recognizing their rights based on specific national and international legislation. Common intellectual property intangible assets include (Cohen, 2005) copyrights, trademarks, patents, industrial design rights, and trade secrets. There is, however, a growing interest in intellectual property management in libraries and the development of specific library and archive international legislation. The Standing Committee on Copyright and Related Rights (SCCR/18) of the World Intellectual Property Organization (WIPO) continues to discuss exceptions and limitations for libraries and archives in a globalized manner (Fernandez-Molina and Guimaraes, 2009), while through the World Copyright Treaty,[1] the WIPO promotes the harmonization of national and European laws on copyright infringement within digital environments.

The intellectual rights management of various intangibles within a digital library environment is significantly different to that of intangible asset copyrights in a conventional library (Mahesh and Mittal, 2009). Technological advances make it possible for digital content to be copied extensively without the copyright owner's knowledge, without intermediaries, and allowing the transmission and use by multiple users. Digital content or content that has been digitized and is available on the Internet is protected by copyright laws, regardless of its original form. The digitization of out-of-copyright material is undertaken by libraries to preserve old, brittle, and crumbling documents for posterity and is not presenting any problems. In other cases, copyright law and interests in protecting intellectual property can affect recorded sound preservation as stated by the National Recording Preservation Board of the Library of Congress[2] and:

> . . . copyright law might be amended, or simple licensing mechanisms need to be developed, to bring rightful protection of intellectual property into better balance with digital technology, thereby furthering the interests of recorded sound preservation. The availability of otherwise out-of-print commercial recordings, coupled with expectations fostered by the Internet that access should be immediate, are at the foundation of tensions between rights holders and users.

On the other hand, library intangible assets may exist when libraries are developing digital content and protecting the digitized material with the use of technology, such as digital watermarking, digital signatures, encryption, etc. to control infringement within a digital environment.

Intellectual property rights legislation may protect public organizations and enterprises within the knowledge-based economy. The value of intellectual property rights (such as copyrights, patents, and trademarks), as well as databases, brands, organizational techniques, and employee knowledge, experience, and relationships, may constitute as much as two-thirds of the organization's total value.[3] Libraries and archives are like no other organization or business in terms of information and knowledge use. The uniqueness of libraries and archives as regards intellectual property rights has been extensively discussed in the literature. In addition, international library associations and other international and national organizations make available certain statements[4] and practices,[5] in an effort to regulate intellectual property rights and issue exceptions for a variety of intangible assets related to library material such as musical, literary, scholarly, dramatic and artistic work, symbols, designs, etc. As stated by the Library Copyright Alliance (LCA),[6] which includes members such as the American Library Association (ALA), the Association of Research Libraries (ARL), and the Association of College and Research Libraries (ACRL), "Intellectual property laws are currently undergoing major changes in response to the growth in the use of digital formats for works" and the library community should make efforts to ensure that these changes "enhance, rather than harm, the ability of libraries and information professionals to serve the needs of the general public." Individual libraries[7] issue various "Library Copyright Policies," in accordance with local legal requirements and the viewpoints of their administrations, regulating copying, scanning, printing, and downloading for individual, educational, research, and general use.

The lack of free access to current literature, much of which is protected by strict property rights in the case of scientific journals, is one of the main setbacks scholars and researchers have to face all over the world. At the same time, economic difficulties are forcing libraries to reduce subscriptions and compromise under economic pressure. One way to move forward would be to invest in human, organizational, and relational intellectual resources—not just for material rights, but to break barriers around information access. This suggestion is introducing the rather significant issue of associating aspects of "openness" with intellectual capital resource identification and management. An interesting analysis of the significance of libraries exploring material freely available within the digital "world" is provided by Smith (2011). On the other hand, for scholarly communication, the Open Access (OA) movement and the development of institutional repositories, where scientific information is being made available without subscriptions, provide additional opportunities for intellectual capital development within research and academic libraries.

The Open Access movement includes a wide number of resources for that purpose. The number of university and research institute repositories (i.e. organizational capital investments) developed for taking advantage of grey material such as lecture notes, technical reports, working papers, preprints, theses, and dissertations is rapidly growing. At the same time, global repositories such as the Open Directory of Open Access Repositories[8] are gradually being made available (Krishnamurthy, 2008). Another aspect of "openness" directly related to library organizational capital is the Open Source Software (OSS). The Open Source Initiative[9] defines the characteristics of OSS as follows:

- free redistribution;
- source code provision;
- integrity of the author's source code;
- free distribution of derived works;
- no discrimination against persons, groups of persons, or fields of endeavor;
- distribution of licenses; and
- a license should not be specific to a product or restrict any other software and should be technology-neutral.

Open source, however, is not free of cost. The cost is being distributed and accumulated in human capital resources (skills development and training, time, etc.) rather than in monetary units. Beyond the cost of development and maintenance, there is the cost of actually using the software and thus the total cost is quite different as compared to the initial acquisition cost, although as Morrissey (2010) suggests, "open source, where it provides the required functionality, and where there is a pool of expertise in its deployment and use, provides very significant reductions in TCO, although it of course does not eliminate those costs entirely."

Open access and open source both provide innovative opportunities for the actual development of various intangible assets that need to be appropriately managed in order to enhance the value of library services. OSS in libraries contributes to the improvement of organizational capital and includes integrated library systems (Koha, Evergreen, OPALS, etc.), OPACs (online public access catalogs—Scriblio, VuFind, SOPAC, etc.), digital repository software (DSpace, Fedora, E-Prints, etc.), federated searching (LibraryFind, dbWiz, Masterkey, etc.), and other library software such as LibX, OCLC Open Source Projects, DCPL iPhone App, and commercial support services. Although the source code is free, there is a cost associated with their utilization including development, training, and maintenance. The final software products add value to the intellectual capital of a library. Similarly, although "transactions" in open access are free, they are not costless due to other issues relating to content evaluation and management, etc. These organizational actions constitute intellectual capital for libraries and therefore it is desirable to focus further on stakeholder views, taking their perceptions into account when making economic decisions and/or investigating specific scholarly communication policy characteristics (Banou and Kostagiolas, 2007). Generally speaking, the OA movement has redefined scholarly communication worldwide. As a result, leading Scientific, Technical, and Medical (STM) international publishers have gradually begun to provide options to authors and organizations for giving free access to their scientific work through Creative Commons licenses. Creative Commons licenses provide simple, globally consistent alternatives to the "all rights reserved" paradigm of the traditional copyright approach. A detailed examination of the effects of the "openness" movements on library intellectual capital, though very interesting, goes beyond the scope of this analysis.

Academic libraries, all over the world, support scholarly communication by developing scholarly intellectual capital. The proliferation of digital scholarly material may cause libraries to form synergies and opt for obtaining the access rights to a document instead of actually acquiring it. Public libraries, on the other hand, are important social capital generators (Varheim, 2009) as they support public sector initiatives. This is demonstrated, for instance, in the analysis of the Spanish public sector intellectual capital provided by Ramirez (2010). Libraries should take part in collaborative information networks. Collaboration (Sheng and Sun, 2007) is based on mutual trust and libraries of all kinds need to invest in "trust building." Some examples of cooperative intellectual capital resources developed by library networks include catalog sharing, interlibrary loan agreements and electronic document delivery systems, technology and knowhow sharing. Train and Elkin (2001) argue that user training programs are important for developing a sustainable and trustworthy relationship between the staff and the users. Such library initiatives may include intangibles such as literacy and reader development programs. A reader development program could contain structured workgroup sessions or events such as Book of the Month club readings or a "Book Forager" game for children. These actions will not only increase reading pleasure and enable shared reading experiences within groups, but will also highlight and promote the reputation of the library, building relational capital. Research on library strategic planning conducted by Pacios (2007) indicates that planning summer reading programs, cooperating with teachers to organize reading events, and developing reading activities for the elderly or children are key actions that promote a library's reputation.

The management of intellectual capital begins with identifying intangible resources to make library services:

- responsive to library users/customers and patrons (develop proactive and innovative services within a competitive marketplace);
- locate, define, and reach underserved communities (developing innovative services in public libraries, employing digital services);
- find ways to resolve all problems relating to access (help individuals with the use of new online technology);
- personal, based on user information behavior profiles;
- embrace the paradox that the Internet (Google, Wikipedia, etc.) is both a competitor and an ally to the library, by developing free online web services; and
- capitalize all types of service points, "real" and virtual, by implementing semantic language search technology and other types of information technology.

Overall intangible resource utilization should aim at making libraries deliver more than popular web search engines like Google do for a lesser or equivalent cost. Significant work needs to be done by libraries in order to make sure that scholarly information and educational and cultural materials are being made available to all users within international, multicultural, and networked information environments.

Human capital

The largest part of a library's human capital is its staff. Library staff training and staff quality in general are very important intangible assets, embodied within library human capital. The continuous training of library staff is a significant factor that promotes innovation and creativity, and ensures that the library is the information starting point for its community of users (Broady-Preston and Felice, 2006). Staff training may cover topics such as advanced searching techniques on databases, using the OPAC, developing information literacy programs, evaluating resources, using e-journals and e-books, and employing certain research methods. The Bond University library scorecard (Cribb, 2005) provides specific criteria for evaluating the quality of library staff. These characteristics include flexibility, user focus, motivation, proactiveness, innovation, and teamwork. Human capital should comprise not only the potential of the individuals employed directly in the library but also of those related to it in any way. It should include, for instance, library volunteers or members of particular library book clubs, etc. A list of potential components of human resources is included in Table 3.1.

Table 3.1 Components for the analysis of library human capital resources

Indicative human resources categories	Examples of specific intellectual capital resources
Competences	Education Work-related competences/experience/staff training Personal networks inside and outside the organization Occupational assessments Specific knowledge and ability areas that include specific skills (e.g. music cataloging)
Attitude	Motivation Team development Psychometric assessments Social intelligence
Intellectual agility	Adaptation Empathy Proactive and reactive abilities Innovation

Source: Modified from Roos et al. (2005).

Organizational/structural capital

The organizational/structural capital may include the library's organizational structure, management systems, collections (both digital and conventional), automation systems, patents, and copyrights. For example, Zhang (2006) argues that contracts and copyrights, digitized collections, and access policies should be accounted for in any digital library evaluation. The dissemination of information is essential for a digital library and enhances its overall structural quality. Library organizational capital includes team organization and learning culture. Sheng and Sun (2007) mention that hierarchical organizational structures (pyramid structures) have several disadvantages, such as poor communication, excessive red tape, conflicts among departments, and a general lack of coordination in day-to-day business practices. They suggest that, in the 21st century, knowledge-based, self-managed teams should be able to overcome bureaucratized structures in libraries. Knowledge-based team organization structures may increase the ability of the library's staff to use their skills and competencies, take risks in developing innovative services, and implement pioneering activities and services. A learning culture environment is suitable for any library since it focuses on good communication, trust and continuous improvement. Mullins (2001) also suggested that the traditional organizational hierarchy needs to be replaced by a team-centered management.

Organizational resources are usually owned and controlled by a library, hence management comprehension and continuous investments are required. Table 3.2, like Table 3.1, includes indicative categories of library structural capital with a summary of intangible asset examples, meeting the requirements of completeness, distinctness, independence, and agreeability.

Table 3.2   Components for the analysis of libraries' organizational capital resources

Indicative organizational resources categories	Examples of intellectual capital resources
Externally oriented	Access to digitized collections Aggregators for information accumulation Agreements/cooperative agreements Brand names and logos Design rights Trade secrets Contracts and copyrights Users' IT literacy Distribution networks Distribution rights Licenses – professional, business, etc. Remote services Subscriptions Trademarks
Internally oriented	Library culture Management philosophy User information/records/databases Organizational flexibility Awards and judgments (legal) Backlogs of library services Computer software (both internally developed newspaper morgue files and externally purchased) Automation systems Designs, patterns, diagrams, schematics, technical drawings Development rights User surveys Library user anxiety Employment contracts Favorable financing/financial relations Goodwill Government programs Historical documents Old and rare material Innovation services planning Insurance in force Internal communication practices

(Continued)

Table 3.2	Components for the analysis of libraries' organizational capital resources *(continued)*

Indicative organizational resources categories	Examples of intellectual capital resources
	Documentation and manuals ("how we do things here")
	Location value
	Marketing and promotional materials
	Art related material and musical compositions
	Content description/metadata
	Collection digitization
	Access rules and regulations
	Permits
	Printed and digital collection material
	Quality/safety management systems
	Repositories
	Strategic/business planning
	Structural organization quality
	Team culture
	Training manuals and related educational materials, courses, and programs
	Users' surveys

Source: Modified from Roos et al. (2005).

Library organizational assets include databases and digitized information content along with an infrastructure developed to provide access to other institutions—for instance, a local public library. Anttiroiko and Savolainen (2007) point out that the role of public libraries is "to serve as mediating and filtering mechanisms in local–global interactions." In that respect, library intellectual capital may include the remote services that a public library might develop in order to provide user access to local authorities and public administration services. In addition, the digitized content provided through the Internet is rapidly increasing. A library can be the intermediate node, collecting information from heterogeneous networks, assessing its accuracy, organizing it, and then providing it to users. User surveys are intangible assets subsumed to the organizational/structural capital. Recent research on library strategic planning (Pacios, 2007) showed that user surveys may lead to important observations that are extremely useful for public library planning and collection development.

Brand names are valuable intangible assets. Anfruns (2009) identifies the brand name, know-how, and assets embodied in human capital, as being vital intangible assets for a museum. Important museum assets may also be derived from franchise agreements such as licenses for using brand names, trademarks, lending exhibits, know-how transferring, or managing a museum. Consider, for example, the significance of the brand name of a museum (Anfruns, 2009) such as the Guggenheim, the Louvre, or the Hermitage. The value of such intangible assets is quite high. The Guggenheim Bilbao, a Spanish museum founded in 1997, paid a franchise fee of 18 million euros (around $21.5 million which is about 15 per cent of the total investment) to the Guggenheim Museum in Manhattan, New York. The Louvre Abu Dhabi Museum in the United Arab Republic, due to open in 2012, has to pay €400 million United States dollars over a period of 30 years to the famous Musée du Louvre of Paris, France, in order to obtain the license to use the "Louvre" brand name. The Hermitage Amsterdam in the Netherlands gives 1 per cent of its annual income to the Hermitage museum of Saint Petersburg, Russia. Branding is embodied in every library's structural capital. According to Hood and Henderson (2005), branding is an important asset for reversing potential negative perceptions towards public libraries. This may be achieved through improving public awareness on library services and activities, thus building user loyalty and enhancing the library's reputation.

Relational capital

Relational capital is embedded in the relationships that a library creates with its external environment, such as to providers, customers, potential customers, other libraries or organizations, and investors, in order to create value. Library relational capital may include its participation in library networks, innovation and digital content networks, professional networks, and so on. Strategies such as Customer Relationship Management (CRM) and Virtual Help Desks (VHD), combined with a Community of Practice (CoP) approach (that is, groups of people interested in a specific knowledge field) are used to enhance the library's relational capital. According to Anttiroiko and Savolainen (2007), in order to increase its value, a public library should participate in information networks with other libraries and create links with publishers and other information distribution and innovation networks. Partnerships developed this way may take the form of contracts, agreements, and synergies through common activities. Table 3.3 provides an indicative number of relational resources divided into two categories according to their direct or indirect library utilization.

Library goodwill and intangible assets

A library's goodwill is a rather interesting concept, with many different aspects relating to intellectual capital. Reilly and Schweihs (1998) identify three different viewpoints that shape a library's goodwill or may explain why goodwill exists as an intangible resource in a library. The first viewpoint has to do with the synthesis and readiness of the library's elements, namely collection, staff, equipment, capital, etc. The functional, operational, and physical synthesis of the

Table 3.3 Components for the analysis of library relational capital resources

Indicative relational resources categories	Examples of intellectual capital resources
Related directly to the library	Advertising campaigns and programs User relationships/user loyalty/trust Reputation Information literacy programs Adult education programs Reading development programs User training programs Information suppliers/publishers Library networks/information networks Partnerships Personality contracts Public relations Technology sharing agreements Users/customers relationships Web enterprises (e.g. Google)
Related indirectly to the library	Broadcast licenses (radio, television, etc.) Economy/unemployment Information policy makers Information regulators (public or private) Local/regional government contracts, programs, etc. Mass media National government contracts, programs, etc. Regulatory approvals or exemptions from regulatory requirements Research organizations/universities Royalty agreements Shareholder agreements Society/special interest groups (relationships, common programs, etc.)

Source: Modified from Roos et al. (2005).

elements creates intangible assets and increases the value of the library. For example, the value of Braille equipment for blind people is greater within an operational library environment than by itself (such as on a liquidation basis) and may create distinctive intangible assets, for example human capital in the form of specially trained personnel or relational capital in the form of relationships built with the community. The second viewpoint is the excess of cost over the assets acquired and liabilities assumed. The third viewpoint of goodwill is the expectation of future events that are not directly related to the current operation of a library. In this perspective, goodwill is developed by investor expectations as regards the future value of the staff, services, relations with customers, etc.

Figure 3.2 summarizes the three distinct perspectives of library goodwill: the first perspective of goodwill is confined within a library organizational setting and has to do with library operations and services. The second perspective can be viewed as a professional practice goodwill that relates to specific library services and practices, and may have two components: the library staff component, which is directly related to the library's staff reputation, and the library component, which is related to the library's presence within the community, regarding location, reputation, longevity, building, services, and organizational culture, etc. Finally, the third goodwill perspective may be viewed as a "celebrity" goodwill

Figure 3.2 Different perspectives of library goodwill

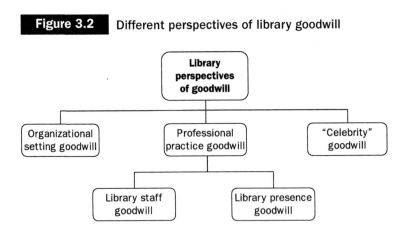

that is associated with the skills and ability of a person to accomplish exceptional professional achievements in the future.

The three types of goodwill are interpreted differently by accountants, economists, and management teams, while different methods are employed for their measuring, valuation, and reporting. A discussion of goodwill financial valuation and reporting in relation to the identification of intangible assets can be found in Mard et al. (2007):

> An acquired intangible asset shall be recognized apart from goodwill if that asset arises from contractual or other legal rights. If an intangible asset does not arise from contractual or other legal rights, it shall be recognized apart from goodwill only if it is separable. That is, it must be capable of being separated or divided from the acquired enterprise and sold, transferred, licensed, rented, or exchanged (regardless of whether there is an intent to do so). An intangible asset that cannot be sold, transferred, licensed, rented, or exchanged individually is still considered separable if it can be paired with a related contract, asset, or liability and be sold, transferred, licensed, rented, or exchanged.

The development of a more active culture for intellectual capital management actions will lead library administrations (Germano, 2011) "to actively convert goodwill to stated value for users that can be established, confirmed and by extension, self-replicating." This change in culture is indeed important for libraries so that they can prove their value and re-emerge from the current economic downturn, along with other information providers. The same author characteristically states: "Libraries need to adopt an ideological shift that moves away from suppositions regarding libraries as inherently valuable." This is certainly the case for the analysis of library intangible asset management, which in our view is providing facts to support romantic notions of the real societal, cultural, or educational value of libraries. A practical and rather simple example for explaining the goodwill produced by a library is provided by Choudhary et al. (2011). Let us assume that the library expenses for acquiring printed and electronic resources are R, with S being the total expenses for the library's staff. Then, the total library expenses (E) are $E = R + S$. A desired outcome for the library would be the goodwill, denoted by $G = SO - E$, where SO is the successful outcomes and E the total expenses for achieving them. Recently, a number of papers have commented on the goodwill created by library operations and services (for example, Sidorko and Yang, 2011; White, 2008; Jefcoate, 2006), while others make suggestions for the creation of library goodwill (for example, Walden, 2006).

Contract-based intangible assets

Intangible resources linked to contracts include a variety of library rights as a result of written and legally enforceable contractual agreements and arrangements. The status of the existing contracts affects the value of beneficial interests conveyed by the subject contract (Reilly and Schweihs, 1998). In libraries, contract intangibles may be established for a variety of agreements between local and/or regional or national entities and the library, among libraries, libraries and associations, libraries and information providers, etc. Reilly and Schweihs (1998) classified contract intellectual capital into two categories: contracts related to receiving goods or services with a favorable arrangement for the library, and contracts related to library financing for the provision of services, securing the library with current or future benefit streams or securing user rights. The first category may include intangible asset contacts such as:

- employment contracts for specialized services;
- items or information distribution agreements with favorable distribution rights;
- insurance contracts with favorable insurance rates;
- services or equipment supply contracts with favorable terms;
- service agreements and operating licenses providing restricted "control" over specific groups of users (demand segments); and
- licensing rights which provide restricted use of intellectual property.

The second category of intangible assets may include a wide variety of contracts such as:

- user and subscription rights for the protection of library user rights and fees;
- license rights for the protection of intellectual property/ royalties;
- branch contracts for securing service continuation outside the main library building; and
- future contracts, service agreements and provider contracts for the maintenance of the library's financing/revenue.

The contracts mentioned above may vary significantly from one country to another and should be further studied according to the legal entity (public or private) of the library and the legal entity of the second contractual party (private or public body, local authorities, non-profit organization, etc). Contracts can be quite diverse and may result from a wide range of circumstances. For example, contract intangible assets may include library outsourcing contracts (for example,

Bénaud and Bordeianu, 1999), contractual agreements for the participation of libraries in various library consortia (for example, Nfila and Drako-Ampem, 2002), contracts for participating in international projects (for example, the Europeana[10] EU (European Union) project), contracts for creating institutional repositories (Kelly, 2007), or even a contractual agreement between a library and other parties for carrying out a state publications Depository Library Program—assuring that a depository library provides digital access to state publications, including bibliographic records for state publications, full text online access through a digital repository, an online library catalog for all digital state publications, and staff assistance for the use of the Depository. Further examples may include user contracts for item loans, renewals, fees, fines, or licensing fees, and royalties that are included in a contract for a music library, etc. In other cases, library contracts reflect a continuation of a long-existing library service for the benefit of all residents of the library district, which is being negotiated periodically with local authorities, city councils, board of supervisors, etc. The library's history as regards contract renewals and the average service life of the contracts, as well as the overall number and types of all different contracts, are issues to be considered when examining intangible assets based on existing library contracts.

The intellectual capital co-opetition dynamics in library networks

Co-opetition refers to organizations and/or enterprises of the same nature that cooperate with each other in creating or exploring markets, but compete in gaining user demand or in resource utilization. In other words, co-opetition arises when organizations and/or enterprises at both dyadic and/or network levels compete and cooperate at the same time. Recent reviews on the different perspectives of co-opetition management studies are provided by Bengtsson et al. (2010) and by Schiavone and Simoni (2011). Although during the past 15 years scholars recognized and studied co-opetition in certain industries, little has been said for library networks. We believe that co-opetition is an important factor for the explanation of various library networks. Although cooperation is easily identified in library resource and resources/asset sharing, competition needs to be further studied. This phenomenon should be examined and analyzed in the light of library intellectual capital theoretical perspectives, like those proposed by Peng (2011).

All over the world, there are a growing number of library networks which comprise two or more libraries and/or other organizations coming together in some agreement of understanding to share common resources (for example materials, information, interlibrary lending, equipment, staff with special skills, collection development, cooperative purchasing, etc.) or aid each other so as to satisfy the information needs of their users, beyond the limits of traditional interlibrary loan services. Library networks are usually created through formal arrangements and may include libraries of different geographical regions and thematic areas. The term "network" is used to designate library networks, cooperative library organizations, library consortia, and cooperative library arrangements. A library network may be a non-profit entity with a specific management structure, budget, and staff, financed by its members and serving multiple institutions that are not under its administrative control. In other cases, an information network may be solely digital, or built through a research project. One example is the DRIVER[11] network consisting of all research institutions in Europe and other parts of the world, which aims at developing an integrated repository of journal articles, dissertations, books, lectures, reports, etc., harvested regularly from around 300 institutional repositories from 38 countries (Peters and Lossau, 2011). The wide range of services and operations (Davis, 2007) provided by the network's head office includes training/workshops, continuing education, consultation to network members, professional collection, collection development, shared equipment and supplies, and referral lists/directories. The services provided by network members include interlibrary loans, unspecified professional development, training/workshops, continuing education, referral lists/directories, consultation to network members, and circulation control. Finally, the services provided by external sources/contractors may include catalog production, physical processing, interlibrary loan, union list/catalog production, electronic mail/teletype, cataloging, and access to online catalogs. In such complicated situations, the rights of the various parties involved are important and should be defined through proper contractual agreements (Deakin and Michie, 1997) or other arrangements for sharing the intellectual capital used and/or produced.

The drivers or motives of co-opetition in library networks can be identified in terms of value creation and value utilization: libraries create value by sharing resources through cooperation, but are forced by competition to compete on outcome utilization. Library network-oriented intellectual capital management requires an extensive analysis of co-opetition among the different parties for the value created/ utilized by intangible assets. Within a library network there are strategic issues of co-opetition affected by the development of individual libraries that are involved in a collaborative effort. Strategically, the long-term plans of each library, within the network, should be included in the overall network aims. Interesting questions on the utilization of each library's intangible resources may include the following.

- Under which circumstances should libraries collaborate with their competitors?

- How can the co-opetitive characteristics of libraries and information providers, such as publishers, be modeled in terms of the intellectual capital utilized/produced?

- Which intangibles from each of the three intellectual capital resource categories are involved in the evaluation of an opportunity to collaborate with competitors and which of them are required to manage this type of collaborative relationship?

- Which are the suitable managerial solutions in order to regulate intellectual capital sharing within co-opetitive networks for network coordinators or members?

As regards long-term results, one can identify intellectual capital issues for both the overall network administration of a library network program and the intellectual capital of individual libraries (and the other participating organizations). Enser (2001) suggests the five Cs for libraries within networks: continuity, culture, competition, cooperation, and convergence. By analyzing convergence, the author provides another important co-opetition aspect for extending the availability of digitally, organizationally, and operationally integrated cultural artifacts within memory organizations/institutions or within memory networks combining librarianship and other subject disciplines. Co-opetition for intellectual capital creation/utilization in memory institutions comprising libraries, archives, and museums is another interesting viewpoint.

Among other interesting points, the issues examined above provide an extended view of co-opetition related to both tangible and intangible assets/resources produced/utilized within a library network. This is called library co-opetitive dynamics and is briefly discussed below. Library network co-opetitive dynamics are different for tangible and intangible resources. Figure 3.3 provides a number of combinations of strong, moderate, and weak scenarios for cooperation (vertical axis) and competition (horizontal axis) specifically for tangible, intangible, and overall library network resources. Interactions within the library network produce certain dynamics such as weak cooperation/weak competition, strong cooperation/weak competition, weak cooperation/strong competition, strong cooperation/strong competition in tangible or intangible resources. Mutually beneficial co-opetition situations are generally characterized by a balance between competition and cooperation (Bengtsson et al., 2010). According to the analysis provided by Bengtsson et al. (2010) on the different tensions resulting from different types of co-opetition in tangible and intangible resources, without the necessary provisions libraries might be pushed towards situations of overembeddedness or distance, or even of destructive competition or collusion. Overall library network management and long-term strategies should not allow tension among competition or cooperation regions, striking a balance (within the middle, moderate, overall region, as shown in Figure 3.3) in co-opetition dynamics.

Let us examine some theoretical examples of different library network co-opetition dynamics. Let us assume that a regional library consortium consists of a small number of public and school (public elementary and middle school) libraries. Let us further assume that the current availability of tangible and intangible resources in public school libraries is low, with some school libraries facing staff shortages and lacking basic resources to support pupils. Within the consortium, public libraries share their resources and provide know-how for enhancing school library services and inspiring the school community. Although libraries cooperate, they

Figure 3.3 The dynamics of co-opetition in a library network with tangible and intangible resources

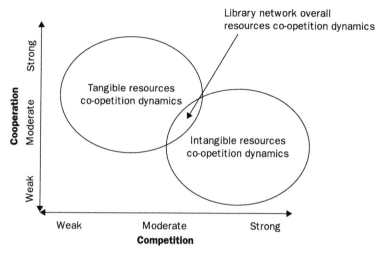

Source: Modified from Bengtsson et al. (2010).

are also competing in terms of resource distribution, public funding within the consortium, and public image. In this situation, the library co-opetition interactions within the consortium are weak in terms of both competition and cooperation, with tangible interaction dynamics being even weaker as compared to intangible interaction dynamics. The latter are more intense due to limitations in personnel skills and expertise demand, organizational aspects and culture, and potential gains in user demand. Weak competition, if it is not a result of choice, may increase passive behavior and reduce motivation for expanding cooperation areas that create future competitive advantages (Katsirikou, 2004). Within this context, library network dynamics primarily arise from the cooperative interaction of tangible and intangible assets. Hence, library network administration can foster competition intensively in order to motivate library members, namely a grand program for using technology in order to enhance school library user services and demonstrate best practices in promoting learning resources within the student community. Innovative management actions can influence network dynamics towards an "ideal" state of co-opetition interactions (in the middle of Figure 3.3). These may include open content bibliographic management services, the digitization of historical photographs or map collections, implementing video streaming and integrating it into the library collection, the digitization of scrapbooks, newspapers, yearbooks, or organizational archives, the digitization and transcription of an oral history collection, the development of mobile technologies for handheld devices that improve access to library resources, and the development of social networking applications for library users and discovery tools that integrate library resources.

Let us further assume, in another situation, that strong interactions in terms of both cooperation and competition may arise within a library network as, for example, in networks of research or academic libraries with other information institutions and publishers.[12] Additionally, the managements of academic libraries, due to significant budget cuts, need to re-examine the role of academic libraries and what they should do differently in order to foster teaching, learning, and research. For that purpose, the support of publishers and other information players is crucial in order to face the library's economic challenges. Strong dynamics stimulate libraries and other institutions into strong cooperation but at the same time into competing actively for scarce resources. Although price is not the only factor used to determine acquisitions, individual libraries or the network's administration may promote mutually beneficial relationships with publishers, thus lowering prices and improving efficiency (Barnes et al., 2005). At the same time, as was suggested over a decade ago, the digital environment provides an innovative competitive environment for academic libraries and publishers, which may in turn enable library users to bypass libraries in favor of publishers (Odlyzko, 1999). As the same author characteristically states, "Librarians will have to compete to retain their pre-eminence as information specialists."

"Openness" should also be treated as an additional tension factor that influences the nature of competition (and cooperation) between libraries and publishers or between repositories and journals (Banou and Kostagiolas, 2007; Brown, 2010). Furthermore, socioeconomic issues, language, and the nature of the digital content should be considered when studying intangible assets within information networks. The evolving roles of academic libraries and publishers within the digital era are producing mutual benefits but also risks that are associated to the development of digital libraries and lead them into fierce competition with each other—as digital publishers (Lucier, 2003). Most of the resources at stake belong to the intellectual sphere of the new economy. Now, it is possible for libraries to act as digital publishers and for publishers to assume new roles[13] as preservationists and guarantors of long-term access to content. Another example of strong interaction is related to the negotiating position of libraries against publishers or aggregators, for getting better prices when purchasing scholarly content. The strong strategic cooperation and the maturing level of trust among libraries and publishers within networks weaken opportunism. Although the presiding theoretical discussion is very interesting, with many theoretical and practical implications, a detailed analysis goes beyond the scope of this work. The role of intellectual capital resources in shaping co-opetition dynamics within information networks is a very interesting issue for future research.

Location-related library intellectual capital and the location's effect on library intellectual capital

Libraries around the world operate within distinct socioeconomic environments. The location of a library does not only have a direct effect on its tangible nature but also affects its intellectual capital. For instance, specific intangible assets are associated with the library's real estate property rights and other characteristics of tangible nature relating to the library building and surrounding area. Traditionally, such location-related intangible assets are influenced (Reilly and Schweihs, 1998) by the library's view, proximity to a central social area, address prestige, easy access, historical, commercial, or architectural appeal, etc. Although the above-mentioned influences are significant for value creation, they do not represent intangible assets but do influence location-related tangible and intangible assets. On the other hand, the intangible nature of intellectual capital may erroneously imply that the allocation of tangible and intangible resources over space as well as the location of a specific library is irrelevant. In other words, one may suggest that an investment in intangible assets may have the same value, regardless of the library's location (building and surrounding area). The location of intellectual capital goes beyond the library's location. However, library systems and services should be evaluated with respect to all of their characteristics, including the location of the library. In fact, although library tangible assets can be transferred and remain largely unchanged, intangible assets embrace human experiences and interactions, and therefore are rather difficult to transfer. Hence, library services that are similar in nature but provided by different libraries should be regarded as different services. Vasconcelos (2008) also argues that the exchange value of information services, channels, and systems should be studied using "traditional" economic and accountancy methods, but the utilization of information should be studied using a user-centered cognitive approach, considering the user, use, and contributions of information.

It is believed that libraries provide services that are turned into intellectual capital for the individuals and organizations that they serve through the value-in-use of information as described by Repo (1986). The value of the information services and/or the intellectual capital produced by libraries is conditioned by market forces through their exchange value as well as their expected and perceived value-in-use. Nevertheless, it would be rather unrealistic to examine the utilization of intellectual capital for a specific library without considering the library's location. For instance, the utilization of human capital might be significantly influenced by cultural characteristics, active social networks, and different higher education systems. Neighboring scientific and/or academic institutions as well as an urban or a rural location may influence staff quality and the availability of training programs. Organizational and relational capital may be significantly influenced by infrastructure availability or regulations and laws that are specific to a particular country and therefore may or may not foster the exploitation of certain intangible assets. The utilization of organizational patterns of communication, norms, values, and generally all aspects of library and information theory and practice take different forms within different cultural settings (Pors, 2007). The location factor plays a significant role, but its importance remains to be determined further through more theoretical and empirical research in the future.

Summary

In this chapter an analysis of distinct intellectual capital library resources has been undertaken and some more complex topics on the identification of intellectual capital resources have been covered. Each of these issues may provide an excellent motive for further research on the subject leading to additional theoretical and practical results. For example, each of the different intellectual capital resources can be further analyzed and examined on the basis of its effect on value creation for different types of libraries, under distinct socioeconomic conditions, using theoretical and empirical research methods. A number of very interesting associations concerning intellectual capital were made, including intellectual property rights, the open access movement, library goodwill, the library's location, and competition and cooperation (co-opetition) within library networks. No attempt was made to describe in detail the above-mentioned library intellectual capital management perspectives, although the research possibilities are clearly very broad.

Notes

1. *www.wipo.int/treaties/en/ip/wct/trtdocs_wo033.html*
2. *www.clir.org/pubs/reports/pub148/pub148.pdf*
3. *www.sonecon.com/docs/studies/0807_thevalueofip.pdf*
4. *www.ifla.org/files/clm/statements/statement-of-principles-sccr20.pdf*
5. *http://librarycopyright.net/digitalslider, www.librarylaw.com/ Copyright_and_Libraries.html*
6. *www.librarycopyrightalliance.org/index.shtml*
7. For example, *www.umuc.edu/library/libhow/copyright.cfm*
8. OpenDOAR—*www.opendoar.org*

9. The Open Source Initiative: *www.opensource.org/docs/ definition.php*, 2004. Version 1.9
10. *www.version1.europeana.eu/web/europeana-project*
11. *www.driver-repository.eu*
12. *http://eyetoeye.ingenta.com/library/issue24/insight-lib-comp. htm*
13. *www.scribd.com/doc/55251004/Convergence-and-Divergence-among-Digital-Libraries-and-the-Publishing-Industry*

4

Measuring libraries' intellectual capital

Abstract: The first three chapters provided an overview of the concepts related to the management of library intellectual capital. Chapter 1 included concepts, definitions, and intellectual capital categorization methods, Chapter 2 provided a historical overview of the diachronic presence and significance of intangibles, and Chapter 3 attempted an analysis of intangible identification. Over the past 30 years, a great number of intellectual capital measurement approaches have been introduced. All these methods differ in their conceptualization, measurement approach, and philosophy. Furthermore, there is not a single universally accepted measurement method applied generally or for libraries in particular. In this chapter, an analysis of the indices related to library intellectual capital measurement is attempted and two prevalent scorecard methods (the Balanced Scorecard and the Skandia Navigator) are presented. Suggestions for weighting the relative importance of intangible resource categories and a framework for creating an intellectual capital hierarchy are also included.

Key words: measurement methods, Balanced Scorecard, Skandia Navigator, analytic hierarchy methods.

Introduction

The previous chapter provided an analysis of the identification of intangible assets in libraries. In this chapter, several methodologies for measuring library intellectual capital will be introduced and discussed. Although the assertion that "what is measured is managed" is quite trite, it still remains very important. This assertion should make the question "why measure library intangibles?" worth asking but rather self-evident. Intellectual capital, however, is difficult and expensive to measure, and the results are uncertain (Sveiby, 2010). Some well-established methods have been developed in order to serve this purpose. On the other hand, libraries all around the world have some very good reasons for measuring their intellectual capital, since it might prove to be very important for their sustainability and competitive advantage. There have been, however, very few theoretical and practical results available up to now. Perhaps this delay is a result of the difficulties inherited in this particular economic sector. For example, measuring customer satisfaction, loyalty, and other customer-related attributes requires an identification of the library's "customers." However, assuming, for example, that active users are the only "customers" of a public library is only one part of the story, since it relates to only one library output (such as loans and visitations). The "customers" of the library's events and other social interactions (cultural events, etc.) are difficult to examine and survey. These additional sector-specific difficulties also need to be addressed when measuring intellectual capital in libraries.

It might be useful, however, before proceeding any further, to distinguish between measurement and valuation (financial or value assessment) methods. The decisive criteria for the valuation or the measurement of intangible assets are being implemented through the use of particular metrics, indices, and variables so as to express their quantity and quality. These may or may not be expressed in monetary terms. For example, one may or may not use money as an

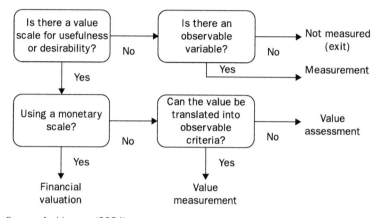

Figure 4.1 Differences between financial valuation, value measurement/value assessment, and measurement

Source: Andriessen (2004).

implementation criterion when measuring a particular intangible resource (Andriessen, 2004). Figure 4.1 shows the existing relationship between financial valuation, value measurement, value assessment, and resource measurement. Hence, for each intellectual capital resource measurement and for each valuation attempt, one needs to decide whether there is a metric (or an index) for a particular intellectual resource that reflects its value (namely its usefulness or its desirability) and whether this metric should be or needs to be expressed in monetary terms or other observable performance criteria.

Poll (2007) provides a review of library resource benchmarking, making reference to a wide range of performance measurement indicators that are used in national- and regional-scale projects. On the other hand, Ross et al. (1998), for instance, as quoted in Liebowitz and Suen (2000), propose a number of metrics for intellectual capital, as follows.

- Human capital:
  - percentage of employees with higher education degrees;
  - IT literacy;
  - hours/training of employee/year;
  - average duration of employment;
  - hours spent in debriefing;
  - hours spent by higher-ranking staff for explaining strategy and actions to other staff members;
  - leadership index;
  - motivation index;
  - savings from implementing employee suggestions;
  - new actions implemented through suggestions;
  - background variety index (at an individual and group level);
  - company diversification index.

- Structural capital:
  - percentage of supplier/customer business accounted for;
  - length of relationship;
  - partner satisfaction;
  - customer retention;
  - management expenses over total revenues;
  - revenues from patents/software/data/databases, etc.;
  - processes completed without error;
  - percentage of business from new products;
  - training efforts—expenses/employee hours;
  - renewal expenses/operating expenses;
  - new patents/software development, etc.

Some of the elements mentioned above may be expressed in monetary terms (for example, management expenses over total revenues) while others are expressed through specific metrics, the level of which can then be observed, namely measured (for example percentage of employees with higher education degrees user satisfaction, etc.). In this chapter, we will focus on measurement, and in the following chapter, we will center upon valuation methods. Some general metrics and other sector-specific elements have been developed by professionals and researchers over the years and were used for measuring intellectual capital in individual companies or on a wider scale. The methods developed comprise sets of metrics or their combinations in order to satisfy the needs of a specific measurement setting.

The next paragraph provides a general background to intellectual capital metrics and measurement methods that are commonplace in the literature of this field. Thereafter, the most suitable methods, adjusted to the environment of libraries, are reviewed in more detail. For the purposes of measurement, some direct and indirect metrics are required, which should be easily accessible in every library. Furthermore, a framework for the identification of a hierarchy among the three intangible resource categories (human, organizational/structural, and relational capital) with respect to their contributions to the library's value creation is discussed. The framework proposed below is based on an Analytical Hierarchy Process (AHP) and a Delphi method as well as on international standards such as the ISO 11620 and the ISO/TR 20983. The hierarchy weights are then employed as linear coefficients in composite indices, measuring the overall performance of a library subject to their intellectual capital resources utilization.

Metrics and measurement methods for intellectual capital

Metrics, indices, and measurement methods provide evidence-based intellectual capital management. For that purpose, a great number of different metrics and measurement frameworks have been developed and presented in the literature. Some approaches result from the fields of accounting and finance, and others from management science. However, it is very difficult for accounting purposes to bypass the generally accepted accounting practices and standards in order to include intellectual capital metrics (Lev, 2001). There are three major lines of scientific approaches in the debate about measuring, valuation, and reporting identified in the literature: the managers, the accountants, and the analysts. Although accountant methods and the balance sheet should not be ignored, they provide a rather restricted viewpoint of intellectual capital metrics and measurement. Accounting standards, in particular, are discussed among others in Cohen (2005). The author suggests that a distinction of whether or not an intangible is identifiable is very important since "unidentifiable assets cannot be acquired singly" and accounting methods tend to focus on "fair" value estimation as if an asset transaction would follow. An accounting-oriented strategy, for example, could be employed in order to include intellectual capital value in the following formula for the market value:

Market Value (MV) = Book Value (BV)
+ Intellectual Capital (IC),

where Book Value (BV) = Monetary Value (MV) + Physical Value (PV); and Intellectual Capital (IC) = Human Capital (HC) + Structural Capital (SC) + Relational Capital (RC). Some authors indicate that there is a need to measure intellectual capital only when BV is less than MV (van

Deventer, 2002). However, this approach, as expressed in the equation provided above, is rather simplistic. Andriessen (2004) suggests that the variables are not separable, as required by the equation—namely BV, which is partly dependent upon retained earnings and involves intellectual capital. Andriessen explains that the balance sheet does not intend to approximate MV and not only is there no need to make book value equal to market value, but it is actually impossible. The same author correctly concludes that "The book value represents the historic value of the assets of a company not yet amortized. The market value is equal to the perceived present value of the future cash flow of the company."

In another approach, the differences between market value and the value presented in the balance sheet are expressed through the well-known Tobin's q index: MV = q × BV. Thus, for example, a value of q = 10 indicates that MV is ten times higher than BV. Measuring, valuing, and reporting methods need to be treated separately and complementarily to financial data, going beyond the balance sheet, because it is not always feasible to include intellectual capital measurements within various accounting frameworks (Kaplan and Norton, 2001). Most of the accounting systems are designed mainly for measuring and reporting traditional assets (monetary and physical), hence only a portion of the "real" balance sheet of an organization remains visible (Talukdar, 2008). The visible and the invisible part of the balance sheet, and therefore the need to go beyond the value estimated in the balance sheet, are presented in Figure 4.2, a typical balance sheet.

The darker solid line separates what appears to be the visible part from the invisible part (below the solid line). In the first column of Figure 4.2, it is suggested that the invisible part of the balance sheet is related to the three categories of intellectual capital resources, while the liabilities column of Figure 4.2 contains the invisible equity. Approaches of this

Figure 4.2 The invisible balance sheet due to the presence of intellectual capital

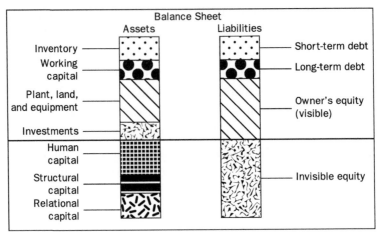

Source: Talukdar (2008).

nature are more suitable for profit organizations, usually belonging to the private sector, while most libraries are non-profit or public organizations.

Intellectual capital measurement methods go beyond the visible part of the balance sheet and are employed for a variety of reasons, including the enhancement of the strategic performance of description capability (Bontis, 2001). They are intended to reflect the whole performance of an enterprise or an organization, providing insights into core drivers of competitive advantages. Furthermore, Jones et al. (2009) argue that knowledge organizations, such as universities—and for that matter a library—include several basic and essential operations for the creation, extraction, and transmission of intellectual capital. In the same vein as Jones et al. (2009), one can argue that for these organizations—such as educational institutions, libraries, archives, museums, and other memory institutions—the identification, measurement, valuation, and reporting of intellectual capital constitute an essential aspect for undertaking a "dialog" with the local, state, national, and international economies and societies.

Another issue for the selection and employment of any measuring method, even the traditional accounting ones, is how to bridge the gap between the outcome expectations of those who conduct the measurement approach and the abilities of the method itself. Therefore, before launching any intellectual capital measurement initiative, one should clarify whether it is intended for internal or external use and other issues related to specific measurement purposes (Sveiby, 2010). Due to the vast variety of existing viewpoints and intentions, a quite extended assortment of different general measurement methods have been suggested in the literature (e.g. Andriessen, 2004; Sveiby, 2010). A quite popular classification method for the different measuring approaches includes the following four categories (for example Roos et al., 2005; Sveiby, 2010):

1. Direct Intellectual Capital methods (DIC) for estimating the monetary value of intangible assets by identifying their various components which can then be directly evaluated, either individually or as an aggregated coefficient.

2. Market Capitalization Methods (MCM) for calculating the difference between a company's market capitalization and its stockholders' equity as the value of its intellectual capital or intangible assets.

3. Return On Assets methods (ROA) where the average pre-tax earnings of a company for a specific time period are divided by its average tangible assets and then the difference to its industry average is multiplied by the company's average tangible asset value to calculate the average annual earnings from intangibles. Annual earnings from intangibles are then divided by the company's average cost of capital (or an interest rate) in order to reach an estimation of intellectual capital value.

4. Scorecard Methods (SC) where intangible assets or intellectual capital components are identified and indicators and indices are generated and reported in scorecards.

All the above-mentioned methods have advantages and disadvantages, especially in terms of their ability to illustrate the financial value of specific intangible resources. A review of some intellectual capital measurement methods is provided in Table 4.1, classifying the different measurement methods under the above-mentioned categories. Although Table 4.1 includes most well-recognized measurement methods, it is not intended to be extensive. What is more, in the literature, different authors classify some of the measurement methods under different categories or identify their creation and development in other bibliographical sources. It is also true that all intellectual capital prominent researchers—such as Sveiby (1997a), Sullivan and Sullivan (2000), Lev (2001), Stewart (2001), Bontis (2002), Roos et al. (2005), Andriessen (2005), Mouritsen (2009), and others presented in Table 4.1—offer in their work their own measurement methods. For example, Andriessen (2004) provides a review of 25 valuation and measurement methods.

Most of the intellectual capital measurement approaches found in the literature differ in their perception, measurement techniques, and other features. Furthermore, there is not a single universally accepted measurement method either generally or for libraries in particular. The measurement methods introduced during the 1990s are mostly scorecard methods based on intellectual capital indicators for capturing the organization's value creation. It should be noted that these methods were extended to include the impact on long-term business performance and are still popular and considered to be well recognized. The methods introduced in the first decade of the new century are striving to associate intellectual capital resources with the organization's performance. Thereafter,

Table 4.1 A review of intellectual capital measurement methods

Direct intellectual capital (DIC)	Market capitalisation method (MCM)	Return on assets (ROA)	Structural capital (SC)
Dynamic monetary model, Milost (2007)	EVVICAE™, McCutcheon (2008)	Knowledge Capital Earnings, Lev (1999)	Knowledge Dispersion Index (KDI), Dhilon (2011) ICU Report, Sanchez et al. (2009)
FiMIAM, Rodov and Leliaert (2002)	Investor assigned market value (IAMV™)	Economic Value Added (EVA™),[3] Stern and Stewart (1997)	Regional Intellectual Capital Index (RICI), Schiuma, Lerro, Carlucci (2008)
The Value Explorer™ Andriessen and Tiessen (2000)	Calculated Intangible Value, Stewart (1997)	Value Added Intellectual Coefficient (VAIC™),[4]	Intellectus model SICAP (2004)
Total Value Creation, TVC™, Anderson and McLean (2000)	The Invisible Balance Sheet, Sveiby (ed. 1989)	Value Added Intellectual Coefficient (VAIC™),[4] Pulic (1997; 1998; 2000)	IAbM (2004) Japanese Ministry of Economy, Trade and Industry
Intellectual Asset Valuation, Sullivan (2000)	The "Konrad" group		National Intellectual Capital Index, Bontis (2004)
Inclusive Valuation Methodology (IVM), McPherson and Pike (2001)	Tobin's q,[2] Tobin James		Topplinjen/Business IQ[5] IC-dVAL™, Bonfour (2003)

(Continued)

Table 4.1 A review of intellectual capital measurement methods (*continued*)

Direct intellectual capital (DIC)	Market capitalisation method (MCM)	Return on assets (ROA)	Structural capital (SC)
Accounting for the Future (AFTF),[1] Nash, H. (1998)			Danish guidelines,[6] Mouritzen, Bukh et al. (2003)
Technology Broker, Brooking (1996)			IC Rating™ of Intellectual Capital Sweden,[7] Edvinsson (2002)
Citation-Weighted Patents, Dow Chemical (1996)			Value Chain Scoreboard™, Lev, B. (2001)
			MERITUM Guidelines (2002)
Human Resource Costing and Accounting (HRCA 1), Johansson (1996)			Intangible assets statement, Garcia (2001)
			Knowledge Audit Cycle, Schiuma and Marr (2001)
Human Resource Costing and Accounting (HRCA 2), Johansson et al. (2009)			Value Creation Index (VCI),[8] Baum et al. (2000)
			IC[9]-Index™, Roos et al. (1997)
			Holistic Accounts,[10] Rambøll Group

Human Resource Costing and Accounting (HRCA), Flamholtz (1985)	Skandia Navigator™, Edvinsson and Malone (1997)
	Intangible Assets Monitor, Sveiby (1997b)
	Balanced Scorecard,[11] Kaplan and Norton (1992)

Main source: Sveiby (2010).

Notes:

1. *http://home.sprintmail.com/~humphreynash/future_of_accounting.htm*
2. *http://en.wikipedia.org/wiki/Tobin's-q*
3. *www.sternstewart.com/?content=proprietaryandp=eva and http://lipas.uwasa.fi/~ts/eva/eva.html*
4. *www.vaic-on.net/start.htm*
5. *www.humankapitalgruppen.no*
6. *http://en.vtu.dk/publications/2003s4hintellectual-capital-statements-the-new-guideline*
7. *www.intellectualcapital.se/Default.aspx?page=17*
8. *www.forbes.com/asap/2000/0403/140.html*
9. *www.intcap.com*
10. *www.ramboll.com*
11. *www.balancedscorecard.org*

some efforts are made for the development of synthesized overall intellectual capital indices such as the IC-Index, the IC-Rating, etc. Obviously, a detailed analysis of all existing measurement methods for libraries would go beyond the scope of this work and is rather unnecessary. In the following paragraphs, a discussion on metrics (and indices) related to library intellectual capital measurement is presented along with two prevalent scorecard methods (the Balanced Scorecard and the Skandia Navigator). Finally, suggestions for weighting the relative importance of intangible resource categories are provided, combined with a framework for the creation of an intellectual capital resource hierarchy.

Metrics for library intellectual capital measurement

As we have seen, although a significant amount of effort has been devoted to the development of intellectual capital measurement methods, very little research has taken place as regards the measurement of intellectual capital in libraries. In this section, we present two well-established methods for libraries that are suitable for non-profit organizations. These methods are simple to use and due to their wide recognition, they can be used for purposes internal or external to the library. When employed internally, measurement focuses on deducing the most appropriate management actions for achieving the library's aims, while external use should address stakeholder perceptions on the library's contribution. These are the Balanced Scorecards developed by Kaplan and Norton (1992) and the Skandia Navigator by Edvinsson and Malone (1997). These two measurement systems belong to the scorecard family of approaches, while the first has been used extensively in the library area.

Another issue that needs to be addressed regards the identification of intangible resource metrics or indicators that can be used for measuring the different activities, contributions, impact or resources. However, as noted before (and presented in Figure 4.1), in order to conduct intellectual capital measurements, regardless of the method used, a group of metrics or indices is required so as to express the quantity or the quality of the library's intellectual capital resources. In other words, metrics are required for measuring the intangibles presented in Tables 3.1 (page 63), 3.2 (page 65), and 3.3 (page 69) in Chapter 3. The Danish Ministry of Science, Technology and Innovation issued a revised version of guidelines for intellectual capital statements (DMSTI, 2003) consisting of four parts.

1. Part 1 provides introductory information on the intellectual capital statement as a knowledge management tool.

2. Part 2 describes in detail how to prepare intellectual capital statements.

3. Part 3 provides directions on how to write and publish external intellectual capital statements.

4. Part 4 provides suggestions as to how an intellectual capital statement attempt can be organized.

Figure 4.3 presents a method for interrelating library management actions to specific intellectual capital indicators, based on the second part of the Danish intellectual capital statement model. As stated in the guidelines, "Indicators allow management challenges and initiatives to be defined and formalised."

According to Figure 4.3, the four interrelated management library elements represent an analysis of the library's intellectual capital philosophy, expressed for a particular setting/service/co-opetition situation, etc., interrelated to

Figure 4.3 Library intellectual capital indicators model

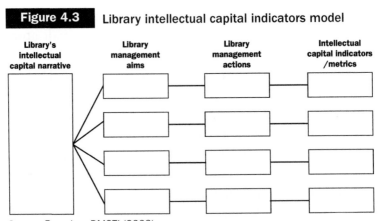

| Library's intellectual capital narrative | Library management aims | Library management actions | Intellectual capital indicators /metrics |

Source: Based on DMSTI (2003).

specific library management aims, actions, and therefore indicators. Some indicators are directly related to specific library actions such as "training days" or "amounts invested in social networking services," while others are related only indirectly to specific actions such as "number of musical librarians" or "newly appointed user subscriptions," etc. Hence through the measurement it is possible to determine whether or not a specific action has been started and to examine its results (DMSTI, 2003). The second part of the guidelines includes some very useful information on the comprehension of the relation between intellectual capital, management actions, indicators, and the role of measurement. Intellectual capital indicators serve three purposes: to specify, assess, and report management activities. Moreover, indicators are generally linked to three different but interrelated types of figures.

1. Measure effects in quality, efficiency, effectiveness, productivity, satisfaction, and quality.

2. Measure the level of intellectual capital resources.

3. Measure the intellectual capital resource mix.

High-quality estimated figures are very significant. According to DMSTI (2003), the quality of the figures is judged based on relevance, credibility, and reliability, while the following questions test the quality of intellectual capital indicators:

- Do the figures relate to the management actions and can this interrelation be analyzed?
- Do the figures provide a fair picture of the library's intellectual capital management?
- Are there both positive and negative figures?
- Are the figures relevant in a way that the necessary information is highlighted and unnecessary data is excluded?
- Are the figures reliable?
- Are the basic data coherent?
- Are the figures accessible by the library (or will they be)?
- Are they calculable?
- Can the figures be reported over time?

The stakeholder relationships, for example,[1] can be expressed through the number and the content of library partnering agreements, the number and the quality of information distribution agreements, the number and the quality of licensing agreements, user surveys, market share, length of user relationships with the library, customer subscription retention, etc. Human resources indicators may include the number of library staff, number of staff in alliances, average years of service with library, average age of staff, full-time permanent staff over the total staff employed, staff working at home over the total employees, staff qualifications (Ph.D. and/or Master's degree), staff satisfaction level (measured with Likert-type scale), user positive effects from implemented suggestions from staff, number of new services and operations suggested, qualitative descriptions of staff (commitment, loyalty, entrepreneurial spirit, enthusiasm), motivation and behavioral indicators, staff training, etc. Other examples of metrics from the organizational capital may include, for management philosophy, the number of internal disputes and complaints, qualitative measures of commitment, loyalty, etc.

Table 4.2 provides some more examples. The first column presents the intangibles, the second includes some statistical data corresponding to each intangible, the third column indicates their financial or non-financial nature, and the last one classifies them under an intellectual capital category. Thus, each metric can be initially classified according to whether it is an intangible or tangible library resource. Then, if intangible, it might be employed to express a specific intellectual capital resource within one of the three intangible categories (human, structural, and relational capital). Finally, intellectual capital can be expressed either financially (Financial Indicator, FI) or non-financially (Non-Financial Indicator, NFI).

The interrelation between the intangibles presented in the first column and the intellectual capital categories of the last column has been based on a methodological approach introduced by Gallego and Rodríguez (2005). Thus, eight intangible resources are related to specific metrics: one of them is classified under human capital (H1), four fall into the category of structural capital (S1 to S4), and three are classified in the category of relational capital (R1 to R3). For instance, intangible asset R1, "Relations between the library and its users," which is classified under the category of relational capital, is related to the metrics "Total number of registered library users," "Total number of active registered users-members of the library's community," and "Total number of users that attend the library's educational activities during every year." Intangible resource S1, "Use of informatics and network technologies," which falls into the

Table 4.2   Examples of intangible resources measures

Intellectual capital category	Intangible resources	Library indices	Item type (*)
Human capital	**H1: Level of staff education**	H.1.1. Number of librarians.	NFI
		H.1.2. Number of library trainees.	NFI
Structural capital	**S1: Use of informatics and network technologies**	S.1.1. Virtual visit sessions at the library's web page by remote users.	NFI
	S2: Databases and documentation services All types of documentation services (e.g. cataloging).	S.2.1. User questions that have been dealt with electronically.	NFI
	S3: Collection informative value The informative value of a library's collection is an important factor for achieving contributions to the wider system within which the library operates.	S.3.1. Size of the library's loan collection.	NFI
		S.3.2. Size of the library's collection.	NFI
		S.3.3. Cost for acquiring monographs.	FI
		S.3.4. Cost for acquiring printed journals.	FI
		S.3.5. Total cost for acquiring electronic information sources.	FI
		S.3.6. Total cost for acquiring printed information sources.	FI
	S4: Operational processes and administration systems	S.4.1. Total library opening hours per day.	FI

(Continued)

Table 4.2 Examples of intangible resources measures *(continued)*

Intellectual capital category	Intangible resources	Library indices	Item type (*)
Relational capital	**R.1: Relations between the library and its users** The number of registered users expresses the diffusion of the library's value (Stewart, 1997, in White, 2007) in that part of its external environment which is related to the users of its services.	R.1.1. Total number of registered users. R.1.2. Total number of <u>active</u> registered user-members of the library's community. R.1.3. Total number of users that attend the library's educational activities yearly.	NFI NFI NFI
	R2: Relations between the library and its suppliers The term "suppliers" is used to designate the publishers – providers of journal titles, as well as the teaching-research staff, students, etc., who provide content to the library.	R.2.1. Number of current subscriptions to printed journal titles. R.2.2. Number of current subscriptions to electronic journals. R.2.3. Monographs that entered the library in one year.	NFI NFI NFI
	R3: Relations with other organizations Interlibrary loan requests and their successful course is a way to measure the value of the cooperative relations established between the library and other library-members of the inter-loan network.	R.3.1. Interlibrary loan requests made by library users. R.3.2. Interlibrary loan requests made by other libraries. R.3.3. Interlibrary loan requests made by users which have been successfully completed by the library's inter-loan service. R.3.4. Interlibrary loan requests made by other libraries which have been successfully completed by the library's inter-loan service.	NFI NFI NFI NFI

NFI: Non-Financial Indicator
FI: Financial Indicator

category of structural capital, is expressed through the metric "Virtual visit-sessions at the library's web page by remote users," while the intangible asset H1, "Level of staff education," which falls into the category of human capital, is measured through the item "Number of librarians" and "Trained library staff." The metric "Trained library staff" is related to intangible asset S1, "Level of staff education," since it is directly linked to ongoing education actions, depending on the position and the university degree obtained by staff members.

One way to move forward would be to investigate the well-known library performance groups of indicators for intellectual capital management. Performance measurement is deeply rooted in the history of libraries (Brophy, 2008) and is based upon well-established groups of indicators that cover stakeholder views and the quality of services provided. Among others, Poll (2007) reviews the literature on performance measurement approaches, while the Northumbria conferences series provides further information on the issue. Performance measurement approaches for libraries include, among others, international standards such as the ISO 11620 and ISO 2789:2003, the IFLA "guidelines for performance measurement in academic libraries," the "New Measures Initiative" of ALR, the "Standards for Libraries in Higher Education" of ACRL, guidelines for the application of best practices in Australian university libraries, and the "Effective Academic Library" guide of Great Britain, as well as various national performance frameworks and European projects, including the CAMILE, the EQUINOX, the EQLIPSE, the PRISM, etc. The management of intangible assets may be further enhanced through the interrelation of performance indicators with specific management actions regarding intangible resources. In that respect, existing library performance approaches might serve as a basis for measuring library intangible assets, if the available data and indices are properly organized, so as to identify and measure intellectual capital resources, as indicated in Figure 4.3.

Balanced Scorecard framework for library intellectual capital measurement

Robert S. Kaplan and David P. Norton are considered to be pioneers in the field of performance measurement. These two prominent scholars introduced an argument claiming that in order for innovation and creativity to be supported properly, non-financial measures should be incorporated, representing drivers of future performance. The Balanced Scorecard (BSC) framework includes four different perspectives (Figure 4.4), which are as follows:

1. How do customers see the organization?
2. How can internal processes and core competencies be improved to satisfy stakeholders?
3. How can value and improvements through innovation and learning be created?
4. How do shareholders see the organization in terms of financial measures?

The BSC framework was introduced by Kaplan and Norton (1992), and in its initial form it did not contain the terms "intangible assets" or "intellectual capital," relying on the concepts of "core competencies" and "critical technologies" instead. A few years later, Kaplan and Norton (1996) analyzed the BSC framework for monitoring progress and acquiring intangible assets for future growth, while, as quoted by Andriessen (2004), Kaplan and Norton (2001)

Figure 4.4 The Balanced Scorecard framework

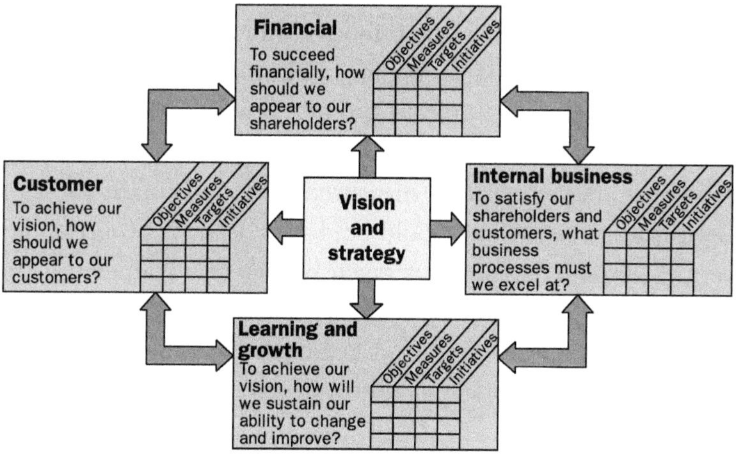

Source: Kaplan and Norton (1996).

fully adopt the intangible assets concept, defining intangible assets as:

- the skills, competencies, and motivation of employees;
- databases and information technologies;
- efficient and responsive operating processes;
- innovation in products and services;
- customer loyalty and relationships;
- political, regulatory, and social approval.

The BSC framework is rather straightforward and has been applied in libraries (Kyrillidou, 2010b) all around the world (for example, The University of Virginia Library),[2] not just as a measurement framework but as a complete strategic planning and management system with an extensive impact on a library's value, regardless of the economic sector to which it belongs (public, private, or social). More particularly, the application of the BSC framework at the Library of the

University of Virginia has received extensive attention for quite some time now and has been presented in the literature (Self, 2003). In the case of a public or non-profit library where the BSC framework is being implemented, the financial perspective can be adjusted to or even omitted from the measurement system. The BSC is a framework that not only provides performance measurements but allows an identification[3] of what should be done and how progress can be measured. The emphasis given by the BSC framework on the customer's view for the library is being discussed in the review of Broady-Preston and Lobo (2011). The application of the BSC framework is as follows:

- the library's vision and strategic objectives are analyzed in terms of the four different BSC perspectives;
- metrics are developed for each one of them;
- data are collected;
- the progress towards specific strategic goals is assessed.

The "learning and growth" perspective includes metrics for staff training and other cultural attributes related to both individual and library self-improvement such as training, innovation encouragement, recruitment, productivity development, job satisfaction, etc. The "Internal Process" perspective includes metrics for service adjustment to user requirements (time and consistency of acquisition and other collection operations, usability testing of library services, service innovation processes, social and regulatory). The "customer" perspective includes user satisfaction metrics (for example, satisfaction with collection, satisfaction with information services, overall satisfaction index, respond to user needs and requirements, convert nonusers to active users, etc.), while the "financial" perspective includes financial data (for example, cost of services, transaction unit cost, donations and external support as a proportion of library expenses, etc.). Examples of BSC strategy maps for libraries are available[4] and designed to communicate their strategy in a uniform and consistent way.

Skandia Navigator for library intellectual capital measurement

Edvinsson (Edvinsson and Malone, 1997; Ross et al., 1997) is actually the architect of the "Skandia Navigator" for the Swedish (Skandia AFS) financial services conglomerate, which was an effort to measure and report intellectual capital, accompanying the traditional financial report to shareholders in 1994 (Bontis, 2000). The holistic intellectual capital measurement model, named the "Navigator," includes five areas of focus: financial, customer, process, renewal, and human capital. The Navigator includes financial and non-financial metrics, defining intellectual capital as the accumulation of human and structural capital. As we have already seen, human capital cannot be "owned" and includes the knowledge, skills, abilities, and innovativeness of the library staff as well as the library's values, culture, and philosophy. Similarly, we have seen that structural capital includes all those things left behind when people leave the library premises and promote the library's staff productivity: software, databases, organizational structure, patents, trademarks, etc. Structural capital also provides the customer with capital which, in the case of the Skandia model, is comparable to the library's relational capital mentioned above and includes all the relationships developed with key user groups and other players. The Skandia value scheme is summarized in Figure 4.5.

According to the Skandia Navigator model, presented in the right part of Figure 4.5, the market value of a library

Figure 4.5   The Skandia conceptual value scheme

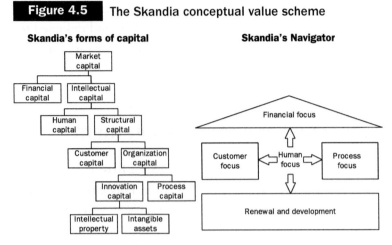

Source: Mouritsen et al. (2001).

equals its financial capital plus its intellectual capital. As shown in Figure 4.5, the financial focus (the financial outcome of library activities) provides information on past performance, while other measurements linked, for instance, to library users (through user satisfaction measurements), human resources, or library processes provide information on the current performance of the library. Finally, as indicated at the bottom of the figure, measurements on innovation and development (that promote the library's sustainability) examine the future performance potential of the library. Focusing on individuals is at the heart of the Navigator and expresses the current knowledge and the process of knowledge creation (educational degrees, cross-training, training per employee, attendance at seminars, etc.).

The indicators employed may be of four types (Edvinsson and Malone, 1997):

1. cumulative (accumulated direct measures);

2. competitive (percentages or indices to compare the library with the sector);

3. comparative (percentages or indices to compare two library-based variables, for example, transactions per employee);

4. combined (combine more than two library-based variables).

The authors initially present a list of 160 indicators which are then reduced to 111 intellectual general capital indicators. Furthermore, Edvinsson (2002) has introduced the concept of the IC-multiplier as the ratio between human capital and structural capital. As opposed to the BSC framework, the Navigator model has a stronger focus on long-term value creation (Neely et al., 2003) through the use of traditional intellectual capital resource metrics, which are dimensionless, ordinal numbers (Roos et al., 1997). The Navigator includes all the resources that contribute to the value of a library, however unique they are, excluding those important for value creation (Neely et al., 2003). The Skandia Navigator model is an equally applicable method for the measurement of intellectual capital resources and their interrelation with strategic library development.

Weights and hierarchy of intellectual capital resources

The measurement methods discussed above provide some form of classification into distinct categories, for distinct intellectual capital resources after their identification. For example, the BSC framework categorizes resources into the four categories presented in Figure 4.4 and the Skandia Navigator provides the categorization presented in Figure 4.5. After the identification and perhaps the measurement of tangible and intangible library resources, using some type of indicator, it might be time to weight their relative significance for the library's ongoing ability to create value in the present or in the future. For example, in Figure 4.6 an example of digital library resource hierarchy is presented, having given relational resources a weight of 40 per cent, human capital resources 30 per cent, structural resources 20 per cent, and all other traditional resources 10 per cent.

Such an analysis should include the different viewpoints of the library's stakeholders and of course different types of libraries may assign distinct weights to different library intangible resources or categories. Roos et al. (2005) provide a framework for making judgments in regard to the significance of the different intellectual capital categories or specific intangible resources, which include the following three dimensions:

1. How influential is a given resource for the library's ability to create value?

2. What level of quality does the resource hold as compared to an ideal situation?

3. What is the quantity of the resource to which the library has access, as compared to an ideal situation?

Therefore, after the identification of the library's stakeholders and the relation between value creation and the library's

Figure 4.6   A fictional example of digital library resource weights

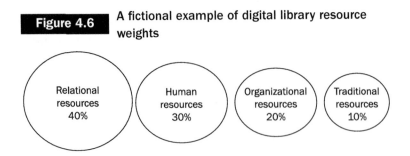

long-term aims, the library's management should organize an analysis, which should include a survey of the identification and measurement of the distinct tangible and intangible library resources. Thereafter, a survey including stakeholders should take place, in order to determine the strategic significance of the resources. The survey should aim at reaching a consensus among the different groups of experts and the library's stakeholders. For such a survey, a formal Delphi method could be employed. In fact, Mullen (2003) conducted an extensive literature review on the implementations of the Delphi method: The number of individuals taking part in a Delphi survey as experts could vary significantly from seven or eight up to 20 people. Moreover, the Delphi method is applied in a predefined number of rounds (phases) and for each round a questionnaire regarding the significance of different library resources is sent to the experts, while all participants respond to questionnaires anonymously. The responses provided in each round are used to evaluate the consensus reached among the group of experts and to define the questions of the next round. During this feedback process, each participant has to confirm or modify the answers they gave in the previous round. The Delphi method is employed for the selection of the most significant library services, which should be included in the different weighting and hierarchy models.

All organizations, and for that matter libraries, are distinct as regards the combination of their resources. Hence, a visual representation of their tangible and intangible resources in the form of a unique distinction tree might be useful. This technique has been introduced and developed by Roos et al. (2005), reflecting library asset inimitability. Library stakeholders are then asked initially to provide the relative importance of the distinct resource categories in line with the strategic aims. In Figure 4.7, the fictional example of the digital library resource representation is further analyzed.

Figure 4.7 Detailed distinction resource tree for the digital library example

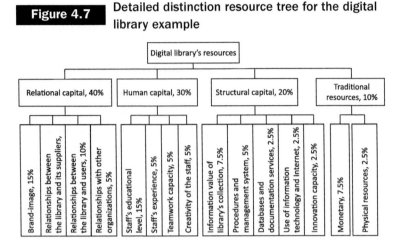

Moreover, if another type of library was considered, a different representation with the human resources as the primary resource category might have appeared. In a second round, the group of experts comprises representatives of the library's stakeholders and would have to further provide weights for specific intangibles related to their significance for the library's strategic aims, within each resource category. So 100 units are divided into intellectual capital resources for each of the resource categories and then the assigned weights are normalized into a 100 scale. Hence, on this level, 100 points are divided among the intangibles of relational resources, 100 points among the intangibles of the human capital resources, 100 points among the intangibles of the organizational resources, and 100 points among the traditional (monetary and physical) library resources. The outcome of this second round might be presented as a detailed distinction tree with the weights assigned by the experts to the resource categories and the specific intellectual resources within each of the resource categories. Following the example of the digital library mentioned above, Figure 4.7 provides the distinction tree showing the relative influence of the different resources on the library's future value creation.

Roos et al. (2005) further suggest that "once the weightings are agreed on, it is appropriate to evaluate each resource for its quality and quantity." For that purpose, the authors introduce a judgment traffic light system as presented in Table 4.3 for each of the weighted individual intellectual capital resources, where green means clearly sufficient, orange/yellow means borderline, and red means clearly insufficient. Finally, in Table 4.3, the resources are grouped together in order to show potential problematic areas. The actions shown in the table are proposed under the assumption that the resource weightings have an influence on the library's achievement capability in reaching its strategic aims, which is analogous to their weighting. Evidently, if for a particular intellectual capital resource it has been judged that quality and quantity are at an appropriate level, then no further management action is required. Otherwise a specific intangible, depending on its position in Table 4.3, might be subjected to further actions for retaining or enhancing its quantity and quality characteristics. Although the quantity of a specific intangible library resource might be understood through the measurement models and indices described above, the quality issue is much more complicated and interesting.

An alternative and rather formal approach towards distinguishing the most significant resources for a specific library is through the establishment of a hierarchy among the three categories of intellectual capital (human, organizational/structural, and relational capital), with respect to their contributions in improving library services and performance (Asonitis and Kostagiolas, 2010). Initially, the library services that are included in the resource hierarchy model for a particular library are selected either by the

Table 4.3 Quality and quantity resource judgment model

Quantity judgment	Quality judgment		
	Green	Orange/Yellow	Red
Green	No action	Ensure that quality does not deteriorate Initiate some quality enhancement activities	Initiate intense quality enhancement activities
Orange/ Yellow	Ensure that quantity does not decrease Initiate some quantity enhancement activities	Ensure that neither quantity nor quality deteriorates and initiate some quantity and quality activities	Initiate intense quality enhancement activities Ensure that quantity does not decrease Initiate some quantity enhancement activities
Red	Initiate intense quantity enhancement activities	Initiate intense quantity enhancement activities Ensure that quality does not deteriorate Initiate some quality enhancement activities	Initiate intense quality and quantity enhancement activities

Source: Roos *et al.* (2005).

management team or through more formal methods such as the Delphi method based on stakeholder representative views. Thereafter, an Analytic Hierarchy Process (AHP) framework is developed and the relative importance among the three categories of intellectual capital for each of the library services selected is derived.

The AHP method was developed by Thomas Saaty (1990) at the Wharton Business School. The AHP measures the relative importance of qualitative and quantifiable criteria, and has evolved over time into an important approach for addressing multi-criteria, decision-making problems of selection and prioritization (Ishizaka and Lusti, 2006). Vaidya and Kumar (2006) present a literature review for AHP method implementations in education, sociology, politics, engineering, construction, etc., covering the years between 1995 and 2003. Uzoka and Ijatuyi (2005) have used the AHP method for library management, as regards the acquisition process, taking into account criteria such as cost, the availability of resources, and the number of copies required. Hsieh, Chin, and Wu (2006) have also used the AHP method to prioritize performance indicators, in order to create a model for assessing the effectiveness of academic libraries in Taiwan. Although the AHP method is elaborate, it is being used to study a complex entity, such as intellectual capital, under a multi-attribute value theory (MAVT) (Roos et al., 2005).

The AHP consists of three basic stages: hierarchical structure creation for the decision problem; pair-wise comparisons (PWC) through a structured questionnaire that yield relative priorities (local weights) on the identified criteria; and synthesis of the relative priorities (local weights) into global priorities (global weights) that lead to the selection of the final decision. In the first stage of the AHP method the decision problem is organized into a hierarchical structure (Sirikrai and Tang, 2006). The first level of the hierarchical structure contains a predefined specific target which should be rather general. The general target is then divided into individual objectives, which are named decision elements (Lam and Zhao, 1998). Decision elements constitute the second level of the hierarchical structure. Decision elements are further divided into a next level of decision elements and so on. The development of the hierarchical structure model is the most critical stage of the AHP method (Sirikrai and Tang, 2006).

In the second stage of the AHP method (Sirikrai and Tang, 2006), the relative priorities (local weights) of the decision elements for each hierarchical level are identified through pair-wise comparisons. Comparisons are based on numerical scales proposed by Saaty (1990), like the ones presented in Table 4.4. The relative priorities (weights) are computed from the data in a pair-wise comparisons table. The data is collected through a questionnaire distributed among a group of experts. This computation can take place either through

Table 4.4   Numerical scale of relative importance

Scale	Definition	Explanation
1	Element A_1 has equal importance compared to A_2	Both elements contribute equally to the objective they particularize.
3	Element A_1 has moderate importance compared to A_2	Experience and judgment slightly favor element A_1 over A_2 as more important to the objective they particularize.
5	Element A_1 has strong importance compared to A_2	Experience and judgment strongly favor element A_1 over A_2 as more important to the objective they particularize.
7	Element A_1 has very strong or demonstrated importance compared to A_2	Element A_1 is favored very strongly over A_2 as more important to the objective they particularize. The prevalence of the element A_1 is proved in practice.
9	Element A_1 has extreme importance compared to A_2	Available data demonstrates the superiority of element A_1 over A_2 to the maximum possible extent to the objective they particularize.

Source: Saaty (1990).

eigenvector-type methods or through methods based on minimizing the distance between the elements of a pair-wise comparisons table and the elements of its nearest consistent table (Ishizaka, 2004). In the third and final stage of the AHP method, the general weights (priorities) are computed with respect to the overall objective (Lam and Zhao, 1998). The calculation of general priorities results from a synthesis of same-level priorities within the hierarchical structure, leading up to the final objective. This process is called the principle of hierarchical composition (Lam and Zhao, 1998).

Figure 4.8 illustrates the proposed hierarchical structure, based on the AHP methodology, as well as the interrelation of the categories of intellectual capital and library intangible assets with library services. The first level of the hierarchical structure only contains the ultimate goal: "improve library performance." In the second level the library services that affect its performance are also included:

1. providing documents;

2. retrieving documents;

3. lending documents;

4. document delivery from external sources;

5. enquiry and reference services;

6. information searching;

7. user education;

8. facilities;

9. collection promotion.

Services that are related to library performance are selected from ISO 11620/Amd. 1 in ISO/TR 20983.

In the third level (Figure 4.8), the decision elements are the three categories of intellectual capital: human, organizational (or structural), and relational capital. Then, in the fourth

Figure 4.8 AHP structure for the interrelation of intangible assets with library services

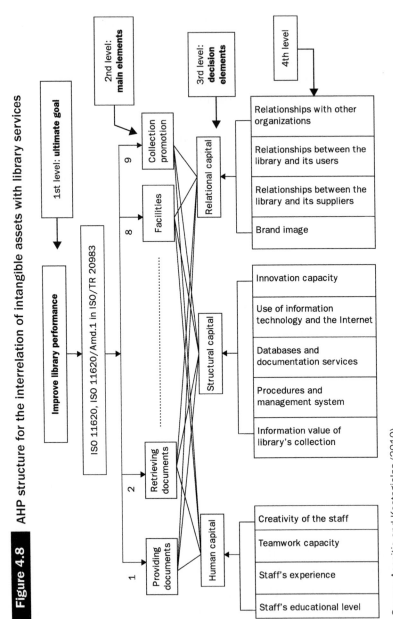

Source: Asonitis and Kostagiolas (2010).

level, library intangible assets that particularize the decision elements of the third level are also included (Figure 4.8).

The number of required pair-wise comparisons (PWC) due to the nine decision elements (namely services) of the second level is quite large. One way to proceed would be to reduce the decision elements of the second level through a systematic method for selecting the most important of the library's services included in this level. The Delphi technique can be used to determine only a subset of the decision elements for a specific level of the hierarchical structure (Miller et al., 2003). Hence the Delphi technique is employed in order to reduce the number of elements in the second level of Figure 4.8. In the Delphi's first-round questionnaire, each of the nine services (Figure 4.8) is judged by experts through a numerical scale extending from zero to ten and expressing the relative contribution of each service to the overall library performance (Mullen, 2003). The Delphi's second-round questionnaire aims at a consensus among experts as regards service evaluation. Standard deviation, interquartile range, and coefficient of variance are used for measuring consensus during the two rounds of Delphi's implementation.

The priorities that are calculated for the elements of any of the levels of the AHP method's hierarchical structure can be used as coefficients for the creation of a composite index (Sirikrai and Tang, 2006). A composite performance index based on the categories of intellectual capital (human, structural, and relational) in the third level of the proposed hierarchical structure could be described through a linear mathematical model of the form:

$$Performance\ index_{(Based\ on\ intellectual\ capital)} = \sum_{i=1}^{3} w'_i y_i,$$

where w'_i, $i = 1(1)3$ is the global weights of each of the three categories of intellectual capital reflecting the degree of contribution to library performance for the human, structural/organizational, and relational capital. Similarly, a composite index for the library services of the second level in Figure 4.8 could be expressed by:

$$Performance\ index_{(Based\ on\ services)} = \sum_{i=1}^{k} w_i x_i, \quad k \le 9,$$

where w_i, $i = 1(1)k$ is the global weights of the k library services selected through the Delphi technique.

The proposed hierarchical creation framework employs a combination of qualitative and quantitative methods, that is, it is a mixed method research (MMR) framework (Fidel, 2008) for developing a hierarchy among all three categories of intellectual capital regarding their contribution to library performance. The implementation of the suggested theoretical framework based on the hierarchical structure of Figure 4.8 is outlined as follows:

- A two-round Delphi technique is used to highlight the most important library services of those described in the second level of Figure 4.8.

- An AHP method is used to establish a hierarchy among the categories of intellectual capital.

- The global weights calculated for the three categories of intellectual capital are used for the construction of the two composite indices for intangible asset categories and services, respectively.

Empirical results based on the theoretical framework presented above are of both practical and theoretical importance for the management of libraries. National and/or regional studies for similar library types, operating in similar environments and in the same time period, may reveal the relative importance of the three intangible asset categories in a particular setting. Hence, the library staff may have an indication based on the hierarchy of intangibles for each particular service and/or for overall library performance. Further empirical results may reveal differences in weights among intangible asset categories in a spatial (for example, different regions, countries) and/or periodic (for example, annual) and/or thematic (for example, different types of libraries) manner. For instance, the relative weights provided for Greek central public libraries below may or may not be the same for other types of libraries, for example, Greek academic libraries, and for other environments, for example, public libraries in the UK. The empirical results presented by Asonitis and Kostagiolas (2010) provide evidence for the relative importance of the distinct intangible resource categories of public central libraries in Greece.

Summary

In the 21st century, libraries all over the world rely heavily on intangible resources. However, the management of intellectual capital requires well-established and practically accepted measurement methods. Furthermore, measurement methods are so important for intellectual capital management that they appear as early as the 1990s with approaches such as the Balanced Scorecard, the Skandia Navigator, etc. These scorecard-type measurement methods have been employed for libraries all over the world and are based on a set of different intellectual capital-related indicators for capturing library intangibles. A next step relates to the identification of the most significant intangibles in terms of their influence on long-term value creation. In this chapter, some methods for providing weights and developing a hierarchy of the different intellectual capital categories or the different intellectual capital resources within each of the intellectual capital categories have been presented. Furthermore, their application in libraries has been discussed, including different methodological reasoning, coverage, applicability of inherited indicators, internal or external measurement purposes, restrictions of use, advantages and disadvantages, etc. The sooner the dynamic nature of intangible resources is understood for libraries, the earlier specific management actions and activities are going to be introduced in everyday practices.

The creation and strengthening of library intellectual capital have also been related to the quantity and quality of intangibles, and are perceived as a part of an overall library value creation strategy. Although such an analysis may be rather complex for an individual library, it is vital and it might make the difference between survival and economic collapse. Even though libraries of the same type, operating in similar socioeconomic environments, may share common characteristics, each library is unique and should be studied individually. Along these lines, future theoretical and empirical evidence based on qualitative and quantitative analysis for library intangible resource measurement and weighting methods in different regions, countries or types of libraries should be undertaken.

Notes

1. *www.valuebasedmanagement.net/articles_cima_understanding. pdf*
2. *www2.lib.virginia.edu/bsc/overview.html*
3. *www.balancedscorecard.org/BSCResources/AbouttheBalanced Scorecard/tabid/55/Default.aspx*
4. The example has been adopted from a presentation entitled "Employing the Balanced Scorecard in Academic Libraries." Presenter: John Potter, Librarian ITT Technical Institute/Grand

Rapids, MI, available at *www.slideshare.net/jpotter49505/ employing-the-balanced-scorecard-in-academic-libraries-1510139*

Presentation of a Webcast Briefing by Dr. Martha Kyrillidou, from "The ARL Library Scorecard Initiative," available at *www.libqual.org/documents/LibQual/publications/ BalancedScorecard_Webcast.pdf*

The University of Virginia Library Scorecard, available at *www2.lib.virginia.edu/bsc/metrics/all0708.html* and *www2.lib. virginia.edu/bsc/LibraryStrategyMap32011.pdf*

A BSC example for library's e-strategy, available at *www. slideshare.net/heila1/using-the-balanced-scorecard-to-formulate-your-librarys-estrategy*

Examples in the EBSCO report of Stratton Lloyd titled "Building Library Success Using the Balanced Scorecard," available at *www. ebscohost.com/customerSuccess/uploads/topicFile-111.pdf*

5

Financial valuation and reporting of intellectual capital in libraries

Abstract: The previous two chapters analyzed issues of identification, categorization, and measurement of intellectual capital resources. A brief introduction to intellectual capital financial valuation has also been provided in Chapter 4 along with scorecard-type measurement methods. Although the financial valuation of intellectual capital in libraries departs slightly from current practices since the majority of libraries are public or non-profit organizations, it is becoming increasingly important for libraries of all types, mainly due to growing economic pressure. Financial valuation and reporting might also be useful for the growing number of private libraries or libraries within private businesses of all economic sectors. In this chapter, three financial valuation methods are initially presented: the cost, market, and income approaches. Thereafter, a discussion of library value calculators and accounting standards is provided, followed by reporting methods for library intellectual capital.

Key words: financial valuation, cost method, market method, income method, library value calculators, accounting, reporting.

Introduction

Intellectual capital incorporates resources with long-term benefits for a library. Scorecard-type measurement methods measure intangibles and identify their contributions to library sustainability. Investments in libraries have to utilize both tangible and intangible resources, and there is no doubt that intellectual capital in libraries and information services goes beyond the financial dimension. Issues related to the identification, classification, assessment, and management of intangible assets, as well as metrics for their contribution to the overall library performance, have been addressed in previous chapters. In this chapter, some issues and methods for the financial valuation of specific intangibles or the overall intellectual capital of the library will be presented. The financial valuation of either specific intangibles or the overall library intellectual capital is not straightforward. The background for any financial valuation attempt is to clarify the objective of the valuation, and identify and prioritize intangible resources/assets.

An additional difficulty lies in the fact that traditional financial accounting standards are inadequate for the financial valuation of intellectual capital. Hence, most financial valuation methods and accounting standards focus on specific intangible resources. As highlighted in the literature (for example Brannstrom and Giuliani, 2009), they include only requirements for the financial valuation of a limited number of intangibles. It is quite clear, however, that the overall financial value of library intellectual capital cannot be estimated as the accumulation of individual intangible valuations. In this context, some financial valuation methods focus on a single intangible asset such as brand, human resources, and patents, while others focus on the system of library intangibles, which is the overall "intellectual capital." Moreover, investments in different economic fields (public, private, and social) create distinct conditions for the overall value of a library (Grasenick and Low, 2004; Gallego and Rodríguez, 2005). In this chapter, three methods of this nature are presented—the cost approach, the market approach, and the income approach—together with a discussion of library value calculators, the accounting of intangible assets, and methods for intellectual capital reporting.

Finance approach valuation methods for intellectual capital

While intellectual capital valuation is a complex problem, libraries fortunately do not have to grapple with solving it. Some financial valuation methods and techniques are actually available and are introduced here. The management of a specific intellectual capital resource takes either the form of a scorecard-type measurement or a financial valuation. Financial valuation assigns a monetary value to intangible resources/assets, while measurement is based on key performance indicators and/or the assessment of stakeholder perceptions about the intellectual capital/intangible asset in question. Three approaches have been made widely available for the financial valuation of specific intangible assets/resources (Reilly and Schweihs, 1998): the cost, market, and income approaches. The cost approach estimates the cost for re-establishing the usefulness of the intangible asset. The market approach estimates the equilibrium price of the intangible, that is, the market price at which the supply of an item equals the quantity demanded. The income approach estimates the future income expected from the acquisition and/or use of the intangible asset, then calculates the present value of the estimated cash flow using an appropriate discount rate. The methods presented below are only suitable for valuating specific intangible assets, since the valuation of an organization's total intellectual capital requires different approaches.

Cost approach

The cost approach comprises several analytical methods, which are based on different cost types (reproduction, replacement, creation, avoidance, historical prices, etc.) and on the concept of intangible substitute products. The most commonly used cost types are the reproduction and replacement costs (Reilly and Schweihs, 1998). The reproduction cost expresses the creation or supply cost for an exact duplicate of an intangible, while the replacement cost expresses the cost for re-establishing the usefulness of the intangible under evaluation. Regardless of the cost type that the evaluator chooses to use, according to the economic theory, cost is not in itself a "rational" value indicator (Reilly and Schweihs, 1998). Cost approach methods initially estimate cost and then formulate an estimation of value, after identifying and excluding all reductions due to the age if the asset. The most common types of cost reduction due to asset age, valid in the case of intangibles, are (Reilly and Schweihs, 1998) operational reduction, technological reduction, and financial reduction. More particularly, the indication for the existence of financial reduction is the inability of the intangible to produce satisfactory financial flows to its owner during its remaining useful life after the evaluation date. The valuation methods of the cost approach (Reilly and Schweihs, 1998) generally apply when the resource is relatively "young" in age and can still be substituted. Library software is an indicative example of such intangible assets. The cost approach might be less effective in assessing the value of older or unique intangibles such as a collection of old and rare books. Intangible assets are considered to be unique when they are very difficult, if not impossible, to substitute and are protected by intellectual property rights, including a trade mark or copyright. The cost approach estimates value with regard to the current holder of the intangible (value to the current holder or owner) and thus it is not of any use when aiming to determine sale prices in a transaction. Some valuation examples that relate to the present holder of the resource are determining the amount of damage for a library after disagreements or disputes with its main stakeholders, and signing an insurance contract for the intangible resources.

Market approach

The market approach includes valuation methods based on an analysis of intangibles that are similar to the one under examination, for which there are recent transaction data available (sales or license concessions). In the market approach, the value of an intangible asset is designated through an "expected value"—that is, an intangible balanced value shaped by offer and demand within a market free of restrictions. There is a general framework for the implementation of market approach methods (Reilly and Schweihs, 1998):

- creating a list of intangibles similar to the one under examination;

- recording the values of these intangibles based on recent transactions (sales, license concessions, contracts, offers, acquisition offer rejections, rights of first refusal, etc.), provided that these transactions fulfill the requirement of independence between the seller and the buyer, and were conducted within a free, non-restricted market;

- choosing the adequate comparison units, based on the nature of the intangible asset (customer, program code line, employee, patent, industrial design, etc.);

- dividing the total transaction price by the number of the adequate comparison units, shaping a value index with the form: $\dfrac{\text{transaction price}}{\text{number of comparison units}}$ (for example, price per customer, price per program code line);

- entering index values in a table;

- adjusting index values (so that they derive only from the intangible asset and correspond to existing conditions and market dynamics). The index price per customer may increase significantly (or slightly) within a highly developing (or declining) market. Furthermore, systemic price alterations in the price index table might derive from reflective or isolated changes in market dynamics. They might include changes in tax legislation, in the regulatory framework for the production sector, in the legal framework for copyrights, etc.;

- classifying adjusted table indices in ascending or descending order so as to reveal price trends that will aid valuation;

- estimating position and dispersion measures for the entire table of indices;

- the analyst identifying the suitable price index. The value results from multiplying the selected index with the number of comparison units. The market approach provides only one value indication when there is only one available price index or when the analyst chooses to do so. In an opposite case, the valuation process provides an entire span of value indications.

The market approach methods may be used to valuate any intangible resource for which there is available reliable transaction data that may lead to the creation of a model or a trend in the resource's market price. In such cases, the market approach is considered to be the most direct and systematic value approach. Intangibles for which there are reliable transaction data are, for example, licenses, trade marks, and contracts with content providers.

Income approach

The income approach comprises all analytical processes of value estimation that are based on future income discount, expected to result from the use or possession of the intangible under valuation. The term "income" may be used to designate net or gross income, net operational income, net income before tax, net income after tax, cash flows, net cash flows, etc. These processes can be applied based on two distinct methods: the direct capitalization method and the discounted cash flow method (Reilly and Schweihs, 1998). Capitalization is the process of turning income into value. Value is the outcome of dividing stable or steadily changing cash flows for a specific time period with the adequate direct capitalization rate (value $= \dfrac{\text{income}}{\text{capitalization rate}}$). We can see that capitalization equals the current value of a stable infinite income. In fact, the method of direct capitalization can be applied only if the future income of the intangible is expected to be stable or vary at a regular rate during the entire time period for which it is expected to yield profit. This time period corresponds to the intangible's remaining useful life and can be either finite or infinite. Some further considerations for the intellectual capital resources financial valuation in relation to the remaining useful life are provided in Chapter 6.

Income capitalization is a value indicator for the intangible resource. The discounted cash flow method is used when income estimation has a defined, finite duration. Expected cash flows can be either stable or unstable for the time periods (months, terms, or years) when they are assumed to be discounted. In cases where cash flows are stable or vary at a regular rate, the discounted cash flow method coincides with the direct capitalization method. The time period is estimated through an analysis of the duration, namely the remaining useful life of the intangible.

Value is estimated through the actual value of the cash flows, discounted through a present value discount rate. In both income approach methods, the most important estimations that the analyst is required to make are related to the amount of the expected income for the remaining useful life of the intangible and the suitable capitalization rate (Reilly and Schweihs, 1998). The expected income may result from the use, possession, or the choice not to use the intangible asset. Income should be exclusively attributed to the intangible asset under valuation, excluding income deriving from tangibles linked to the intangible under valuation or total business activities. For instance, a software company might have developed a new program but may delay its circulation until it receives the expected financial profit from the circulation of the program's previous edition. The remaining useful life of the intangible asset is estimated through a useful life analysis, while cash flow periods (months, terms, years, etc.) are determined by the nature of the problem.

The discount rate in the discounted cash flow method (Reilly and Schweihs, 1998) equals the required rate of return for an assumed investment in the intangible asset. The capitalization rate in the direct capitalization method, for an infinite useful life, is estimated through the relation:

capitalization rate = discount rate – expected income increase. The expected income increase is expressed through a percentage and may be a positive, negative, or neutral number. However, if the remaining useful life of the asset is finite, then the capitalization factor is estimated through the capitalization rate for a period equal to the asset's remaining useful life. Multiplying the direct capitalization factor with the expected annual income provides an indication of the intangible asset's value. The income approach constitutes the core of all valuation theories. Reilly and Schweihs (1998) state that the income approach method is the most commonly used method for the valuation and analysis of intangible resources. As opposed to the market and cost approaches, which operate under specific circumstances, income approach methods can adapt to almost all categories of library intangible resources.

Library value and value calculators

As Kyrillidou (2010a) suggests on the issue of library value:

> We hold these truths to be self-evident: libraries are valuable to humankind; libraries preserve knowledge; libraries enable access to information; libraries serve the information needs of their users. To the believer the truth is evident. But libraries are not natural phenomena like the sun rising and setting every day. Libraries are institutions created and supported by those individuals who hold that these statements are true even if not self-evident to everyone.

Generally speaking, there is an increased need for libraries of all types to develop financial reports—that is, reports that seek to estimate their economic value (McCallum and Quinn, 2004; Holt, 2007). Moreover, the public view for library value deficit (Germano, 2011) should be avoided through a more sophisticated approach that conveys the unique value of the library and its impact on a specific user population.

Some earlier studies focus on return of investment methods (for example, Missingham, 2005) for individual libraries and conclude that no numerical result can represent the true return on investment. Aabo (2009), through an extensive review and meta-analysis of the ROI in library applications, suggests that, on average, they return about four times the value of each dollar invested in public libraries. Recently, Sidorko (2010) and Grzeschik (2010) provided case studies analyzing ROI in academic libraries. Although these models are interesting, questions such as the effect of library intangible resources/assets on the ROI or the percentage that can be attributed to the library's intellectual capital or issues on the financial valuation of intellectual capital were not incorporated. A cost–benefit analysis based on estimations of how much the user is willing to pay for the service, as well as the cost of time saved as a result of their contact with library services, was used by Chung (2007) to determine whether the benefits of special libraries outweigh the cost incurred in providing the services. Another similar but business-oriented ROI approach has been introduced by Pankl (2010) for determining whether a business library is worth being set up: this library valuator is expressed through the equation $ROI = NI - (T + EU)$, where NI is the value assigned by a user to a specific piece of information, T is the amount of money spent on library service taxes and EU is the expense of using the library. Pankl concluded that it is important to convince the top management that there is net value in developing or funding a library within their business.

This same approach can be used to demonstrate library value to local government, in order to be eligble for funds for the local public library.

Library value estimation and synthesis have become more popular over the years and are heavily influenced by the experience and the right judgment of the analyst. Experienced analysts usually combine more than one approach and more than one method in the financial valuation process. As a result, when the process ends, they have at their disposal a series of estimated values—value indicators—for specific library economic value estimations. The final library economic value results from a synthesis of a number of specific financial indicators. Therefore, we could use an equation in order to estimate the value of a library: $Value_{library}$ = $f(I,ITA,INT_{effect})$, where I is the amount invested in tangible assets, ITA is the amount invested in intangible assets, and INT_{effect} is the impact coefficient of intangible investments that affect the library's value. Furthermore, the value of a library could be expressed using the following function (Kostagiolas and Asonitis, 2010):

$$Value_{library} = a \cdot F(I;t) + b \cdot G(ITA;t) + c \cdot H[(I) \cdot (ITA);t] + e(t),$$

where a and b are nonnegative parameters and c is the impact coefficient parameter, so that when $c > 0$, $c < 0$, or $c = 0$ we have a positive, negative, or zero impact of tangible and intangible investments on total library value; e expresses statistical estimation error and is used as an optimum adjustment factor. Time, t, is the parameter that expresses the period in time (for example years, year, semester, trimester, etc.) within which investments in tangible (I) or intangible (ITA) assets were or are going to be made. For instance, as regards the level of education of a library's human capital, intangible investments may have positive, negative, or zero impact on library processes. Intellectual capital investments that aim to improve human capital will have different effects on a digital library as compared to a traditional library.

Over the years, a number of simplistic library valuators or value calculators have been made available. They are all attempting to assign value to library services and thus provide a Return On Investment (ROI) for the user. Such valuators include the financial calculator worksheet of the Maine[1] State Library regarding the savings achieved for library users per month, or the calculator presented by the American Library Association and developed by the Massachusetts Library Association,[2] and quite a few others. As noted above, public library value goes beyond restricted economic results; it is very important for social capital creation (Varheim, 2009) and contributes to the intellectual capital development of the economy and society as a whole (Ramirez, 2010). Criticism of value calculators includes the fact that they are restricted to a superficial user-savings viewpoint and hence they cannot be used for library costing or pricing. Library calculators are restricted to a myopic sense of economic value, leaving out all aspects of intellectual capital that make a library experience unique for each user. The user savings, as computed by library valuators, include only a restricted aspect of value creation which is based primarily on cost avoidance by creating a generic list of prices in order to show how much money a user can save or has saved by using the library, as compared to paying for the material borrowed or questions asked (Germano, 2011). Such library value represents only a portion of the *true* value that the library produces. As Town (2010) suggests, the concept of a *transcendent library* may provide a route to further progress on library valuation, which contributes to organizational and social values, rather than a simple, narrow notion of economic value. The author proposes a value scorecard approach to incorporate both the value and the impact of transcendent libraries in which ". . . the value can be judged beyond immediate needs and demands, through contribution to less concrete aspects of institutional or societal intent."

Library accounting issues for intellectual capital

Ever since 1978, International Accounting Standards (IAS) had addressed the issue of intangible assets. This process led to the creation of the IAS38 standard, which regulates the accounting management of all intangibles, with a few exceptions better addressed by other standards (IAS). The IAS38 was issued in September 1998 and implemented in June 1999. Today there is a revised version (since March 2004) of the IAS38 standard. The SIC32 directive, intangible assets–network projects cost, was issued in July 2001 and implemented on March 25, 2002, with the aim to expand further the requirements of the IAS38 standard, especially for web pages. The IAS38 standard defines intangible assets as recognizable non-monetary assets with no tangible substance. A recognizable intangible (IFRS 38.12) is actually distinct (it can be sold, rented, licensed, etc., separately) or may derive from other legal rights or obligations (for example intellectual rights). Intellectual assets adopt the features of assets—that is, they result from past events, are fully controlled by the owner company or organization, and have the ability to yield future financial profit to the owner. In the IAS38 standard, an asset that falls under the definition mentioned above is entered in the accounts at the precise moment of its acquisition (initial measurement) with the initial acquisition or creation cost (IAS38.72). When an asset is "entered into accounts," it is actually being transferred and recorded into the financial accounts of the company. In this case, permanent intangible assets are recorded in the asset side of the balance sheet of the organization/company. If the asset enters the accounts later than the date of acquisition, then the IAS38 standard allows for two valuation models: the cost model and the adjusted value model (IAS38.72). The cost model is part of the cost approach, while the adjusted value model is part of the market approach.

Figure 5.1 presents the acceptance of intangible financial valuation methods by the IAS38 standard.

IAS usually only partly adopts the cost approach and thus one could not claim that current accounting models are adequately addressing the issue of intangible assets. For instance, there is an important problem in reporting a unique intangible in the accounts under IAS32, such as a copyright developed inside a library, the value of which (as mentioned before) cannot be measured based on cost. Most accounting

Figure 5.1 Adopting intangible asset valuation approaches based on the IAS38 standard

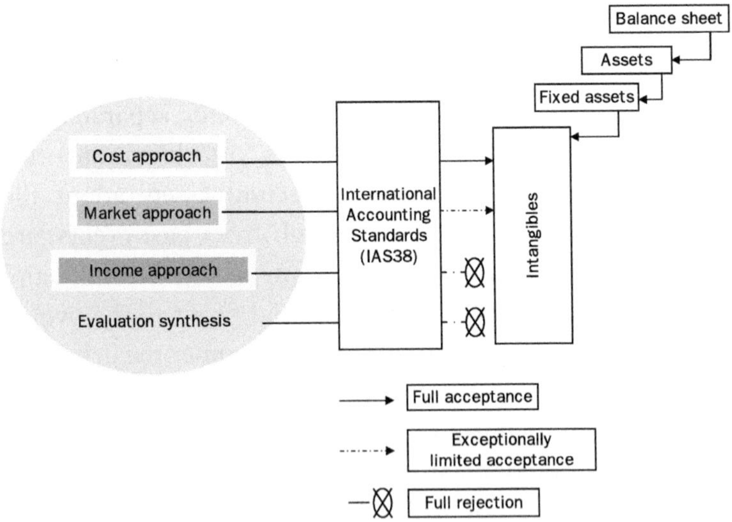

Source: Kostagiolas and Asonitis (2007).

schemes fail to recognize properly intangible assets and they provide a list of specific assets to be entered into accounts as part of the asset side of the balance sheet. Methods for estimating the value not only of a specific intangible but also of intellectual capital as a whole include the discount rate in the discounted cash flow method (Reilly and Schweihs, 1998), which equals the required rate of return for an assumed investment in an intangible asset. The capitalization rate in the direct capitalization method for an infinite remaining useful life can be mathematically calculated: capitalization rate = discount rate −expected income increase rate. The expected income increase rate is expressed through a percentage and might be a positive, negative, or neutral number. However, if the useful life of the intangible is finite, then the capitalization factor is estimated through a capitalization rate equal to the asset's remaining useful life. The direct capitalization factor multiplied by the predicted annual income can provide an indication of the intangible's value. Moreover, the market-to-book-ratio methods adopt a holistic approach in order to assign monetary value to the intellectual capital of a firm. According to this method, monetary value is calculated by comparing the library's market value to its book value. The Value-Added Intellectual Coefficient (VAIC™), proposed by Pulic (2004), also assigns monetary value to a firm's human and structural capital. According to this method, the value added is defined as the difference between the output (total sales) and input (cost of material and services). Human capital is not assigned in inputs, but instead is considered to be an investment. Human, structural, and intellectual capital efficiency are calculated through the VAIC™ methodology. The information required by the VAIC™ can be found in the library's financial statements; however, the method has recently been heavily criticized.

Although traditional accounting systems and related financial reports involve accumulative knowledge and experience collected throughout more than a century for the disclosure of real and financial assets, very few of them address the issue of reporting intangible assets (for example Stolowy and Cazavan, 2001) and can be applied in libraries of all types. Unlike traditional annual financial reports, intellectual capital reports are not mandatory and are used by a minority of firms (fewer than 1 per cent in the private sector) as complementary information to financial reports (Roos et al., 2005). Much of the total value of a library, the majority of investments made in it, as well as its outcomes, are intangible in nature.

Methods for intellectual capital reporting in libraries

As we have seen, the identification of intangibles requires an examination of the library's resources, activities, structure, and day-to-day operation features, from the point of view of intellectual capital management. Measuring the quality and quantity of intangibles also helps the management team to assess the performance and effectiveness of its services, better allocate its resources and investments on new innovative information services, and report its intellectual capital status to stakeholders. One of the advantages of intellectual capital reporting is that it provides transparency to the use of funds (Roos et al., 2005), something that is very important for the library field. As already mentioned, official balance sheets may not contain a trustworthy valuation of an organization's intangible assets. For this purpose, it might be possible that libraries issue an unofficial balance sheet and a complementary use results list for intangible assets, with no tax value but with high significance for the library's management and stakeholders.

Roos et al. (2005) outline five models of intellectual capital reporting:

1. the model proposed by the MERITUM project;

2. the Danish Disclosure initiative;

3. the ARCS intellectual capital report;

4. the Triple Bottom Line (TBL) framework;

5. the Balanced Scorecard model;

6. the Skandia model.

A common feature that appears in all these models is the use of indicators. A set of indicators may contain those related to knowledge transfer, research management, achievement of environmental objectives, customer satisfaction, performance of services/processes, etc. According to Roos et al. (2005), a firm or organization, and therefore a library, should follow a step-by-step approach in selecting the suitable intellectual capital reporting model. Initially, defining the needs of the library is essential. Then, success factors corresponding to the library's needs should be established, followed by a set of appropriate key performance indicators. A draft reporting model should disclose existing data and finally stakeholders (internal and external) should be invited to comment on the report. The procedure should be repeated (in the form of feedback) until consensus is achieved among stakeholders about the appropriateness of the reporting model.

Recognizing and measuring intangible assets within an organization, along with management actions for value creation, should be combined with consistent intangible reporting within the organization, so as to monitor achievement of aims and report back to stakeholders (Roos et al., 2005). For example, the intellectual capital reporting methods of the Austrian Research Centers Seibersdorf (ARCS)[3] could be used quite effectively in the field of libraries since they:

- use the same categorization of intellectual capital into human, structural, and relational capital;
- are based on the use of suitable indices for intangible assets, such as the ones discussed above;
- have been developed for an organization with outputs (studies/researches) intangible in nature, such as libraries.

Using a simple form of the intellectual capital reporting method of the ARCS for the year 2000, Table 5.1 presents a reporting sample for the development of an intellectual capital report.

This simple reporting model employs the usual intellectual capital classification and assigns indices to each intangible resource (for instance, the intellectual asset "Relations between the library and its users" is linked to the "Total number of registered users"). Column four contains the value of each index as shaped at the end of the previous time period of reference (for example year). The next column indicates the intention of the management to either increase, reduce, or maintain the value of the index, using the symbols ↗, ↘, ➡, respectively. Column six includes the index value that was finally achieved during the current period of reporting. The column of "Conclusions" records the satisfaction, neutral stance, or dissatisfaction of the management as regards the results, using the symbols ☺, ☻, ☹, respectively. The final column indicates the intention of the management to increase, reduce, or maintain the index value for the next time period.

Table 5.1 A sample of reporting intellectual capital resources in libraries

Intellectual capital category	Intangible resources	Indicative intellectual capital resource indices	Index value for previous year (*)	Aim for current year (*)	Index value for current year (*)	Conclusions	Aim for the following year
Relational capital	Relation between the library and its users	Total number of registered library users	3.500	↗	4.000	☺	↗
	Relation between the library and its suppliers	Number of current subscriptions to printed journal titles	550	↑	600	☺	↑
		Number of current subscriptions to digital journals	2	↑	2	☹	↗

* Random aims

Summary

Library and information services rely heavily upon intangible assets. Understanding the dynamic nature of intangible assets will promote the competitiveness of libraries. When studying the literature, one becomes aware of the fact that in the economic reality of the 21st century, intellectual capital contributes to the overall value of a library, combined with traditional assets. Therefore, beyond the identification and categorization of intangible assets, an important issue relates to the analytical estimation of their value within a specified time framework. Valuation methods and other analytical approaches may provide an estimation which in turn may be employed for increasing the library's total value. In this chapter, three applicable valuation methods have been discussed: the cost, market, and income approaches. Furthermore, some rather simplistic library valuation calculators have been presented, touching briefly upon the accounting of intangibles. Most national and international accounting systems and other related financial reports mainly refer to real financial assets, examining only a few individual intangibles. A library's characteristics in respect to its intellectual capital resources, especially when they are accompanied by public funding, justify the need to adopt an intellectual capital reporting model. Indicative benefits include (Roos et al., 2005) transparency in the use of public funding, accurate information on the abilities and the overall value of the staff, trustworthy relationships between employees and stakeholders, and finally the ability of stakeholders to monitor the rate of achievement of the objectives set by the library's strategic plan. Finally, this chapter analyzed some important reporting methods, providing an indicative example.

Notes

1. *www.maine.gov/msl/services/calculator.htm*
2. *http://69.36.174.204/value-new/calculator.html*
3. The Austrian Research Centers Seibersdorf (ARCS) is (Roos et al., 2005) the largest research organization in Austria. It has developed its own intellectual capital reporting methods, issuing reports since 1999.

6

Survival analysis for libraries' intellectual capital resources

Abstract: This chapter presents the role of survival analysis for studying the remaining useful life of library intellectual capital resources. Lifecycle considerations go beyond the issues of quantity and quality, presented in the previous chapters, since they incorporate the dimension of time—that is, they involve a number of management activities that should take place throughout the lifecycle of a library intellectual capital resource. The research question can then be summarized as follows: "What is the longevity/reliability of library intangible resources?" For that purpose, some efficient modeling methods that estimate the reliability of intellectual capital, parametrically or nonparametrically, within a library setting are presented together with an illustrative example. From a large number of nonparametric methods that have been made available for survival estimation, only two are examined here: the Kaplan-Meier and the Cumulative-Hazard survival estimators. Parametric methods and applications based on the Weibull distributional model are also examined. The Weibull analysis is quite useful for modeling intellectual capital resources of all three types: human, organizational, and relational.

Key words: reliability/survival analysis, nonparametric analysis, Weibull analysis, Kaplan-Meier estimator, Cumulative Hazard.

Motivation for life analysis of libraries' intellectual capital resources

As we have seen, a significant amount of research has been devoted to identifying, measuring, valuating, reporting, and drawing inferences on intellectual capital resources. This is quite important for library practitioners and researchers, since it helps them understand the way intangible assets function at a given time and thus make decisions regarding management actions. However, the intellectual capital management puzzle should also include a methodological pathway so as to incorporate the dimension of time and its effect on the lifecycle of intangible resources. Reliability (or survival) has to do with the ability of intellectual capital resources to retain certain characteristics after a week or a month or at the end of any given period, for example, an academic year for an academic library. In that respect, although the previous analysis provides a snapshot of library intangible resource status, a survival or reliability analysis incorporates the dimension of time through the involvement of a number of activities and operations that take place throughout the lifecycle of a library's intellectual capital resources. This, however, makes the whole analysis much more complicated since it inevitably requires a probabilistic survival model in order to describe the behavior of library resources over time. This probability model is known as the life distributional model, while Reilly and Schweihs (1998) define life analysis as "the study of the placements of (or investments in) similar assets—and of their subsequent retirements—in order to develop their life characteristics." This chapter deals with the life analysis of library intellectual capital resources.

In today's competitive, globalized information environment, the available quality and quantity of specific intangible resources are not enough. Their ability to retain their characteristics throughout their lifecycle and throughout the library's operations and services over time is extremely important. An organizational capital resource like a catalog, a circulation system, or a reference collection service should be reliable, delivering an adequate service when required, day after day, month after month. Similar questions can be raised about human, organizational, and relational intangible resources presented in Tables 3.1 to 3.3 (pages 63, 65, and 69) respectively. In an ideal library environment, all tangible and intangible resources should be available in a consistent manner when required. The lifecycle of tangible resources comprises their economic life and their service life. The economic life of a specific asset/resource is the time period that this particular resource can be profitably utilized by a library, which does not necessarily coincide with the service life, being the time period within which the asset/resource is used until retirement (Reilly and Schweihs, 1998). Although the economic life and the service life are tied to a specific "owner," for example, a specific library, the lifecycle may include all the different "owners" of the asset and is used to designate the time period that extends from the manufacturing of the asset to its physical destruction. Similarly, for intellectual capital resources/assets the economic and the service time may or may not coincide. For example, a specific library collection item, such as a copy of a textbook, may be in service for as long as it is recommended as a coursework material by the college staff. When, however, the specific collection item is withdrawn from the coursework material, it might still have an economic life, although its service life has ended. Another important pathway for library intangible resource survival analysis models is to study the length of time that an "individual" (user, customer, organization, etc.) spends in a specific situation before advancing to another (Manez et al., 2008). Some examples of such studies may include entrepreneurship survival analysis, the study of employment duration, library relations duration, lifetime duration in regard to the exit of a specific market, and the analysis of the time period for which a library uninterruptedly exports or performs R&D activities.

The consistent failure of intellectual capital resources to fulfill their intended use may significantly affect the library's value, lower its competitive position, have disastrous results. Unreliable resources damage the library's reputation and lead to inferior quality, user displeasure, inconvenience, and lasting user dissatisfaction. In this chapter, we address the following question as regards library intellectual capital reliability: "How can the longevity/reliability of the library's intangible resources be measured?" or otherwise phrased, "How can the reliability of library intellectual capital resources be analyzed?" For that purpose, some background information on life analysis theory and applications is provided and two families of efficient survival modeling methods are presented: the first is based on nonparametric methods and the second on parametric distributional methods. More specifically, out of a wide number of existing nonparametric methods for survival estimation, we examine here the Kaplan-Meier and the Cumulative-Hazard reliability estimators, while the parametric methods presented are based on the Weibull distributional model. These are useful for a wide range of library intangible resource management applications and for modeling user behaviors as well as specific library services and systems (Reilly and Schweihs, 1998; Kostagiolas, 2011).

Survival considerations for intellectual capital in libraries

Survival considerations for intangible resources do not depend solely upon one factor or one parameter. A particular intellectual capital resource may fail to satisfy a set of predetermined requirements, probably due to a number of underlying reasons and mechanisms. These may be different from and independent of each other, although they all contribute to the overall library reliability performance. For example, a library's repository may be reliable while other information services, for example, access to the Internet, may not be. Life analysis is based on the availability of life data and an understanding of the random processes that generate them. The data provide information that involves assumptions on the mechanisms that cause failures. Reliability (or life) data consist of time measurements up to a specific event of interest (usually referred to as "failure"), defined for an intangible asset as the inability to carry out a specific task or to produce specific results, etc. When making a life analysis, researchers define failure according to the needs of each specific study. For example, if one is going to study user behavior over time in relation to a specific subscription service, then failure may be defined as the user's refusal to renew their subscription. In many cases, the conditions that may lead to the deterioration or even to a failure of a specific intellectual capital resource do not depend on the way a library operates and may include (Reilly and Schweihs, 1998):

- physical risks due to accidents, disasters, deterioration, physical wear and tear;

- functional risks due to inadequacy, obsolescence, interrelated resources, evolution technology;

- operational risks due to management, accounting and regulatory policies;

- economic risks due to lack of demand, interest rates, inflation, financing, inadequacy of return on investment.

Moreover, survival data frequently contains incomplete observations, which consist of truncated times to failure; this is usually referred to as censoring. In the previous example, censoring may come as a result of a user's unexplained withdrawal from the subscribed service without actually refusing to renew the subscription. When life data consist of failure times intermixed with random censoring times, we talk about multiply censored reliability of survival data.

Another important motivation factor for a life analysis study is the estimation of the *remaining useful life* of the intellectual capital resource. This can be estimated either informally (based on expert opinions or other judgments) or may result from formal survival analysis methods, which will be presented later in this chapter. Such estimations for the remaining useful life of an intangible resource are, for example, involved in the valuation methods examined in Chapter 5, namely the cost, market, and income approaches. In the cost approach, the remaining useful life is involved in the calculation of value depreciation or obsolescence as the ratio of the *effective life* over the *total expected life* of an intangible asset. Hence, the longer the expected remaining life of an intangible, the higher its value, provided that all other factors remain unchanged. In the market approach, life analysis and the estimation of the remaining life of an intellectual capital resource are important when comparing similar resources or guiding intangible asset sales or licensing transactional data (Reilly and Schweihs, 1998). An extremely short estimation of an intangible's remaining life (say less than six months) might actually indicate small value, that is, a significantly lower value as compared to the intangibles used for comparison. A shorter remaining useful life reduces the asset's significance in the market approach. On the other hand, an extremely long estimated remaining useful life as compared to the comparative intangible indicates high value of the intangible under examination. In the income approach, the remaining useful life estimation is a prerequisite for the valuation process in order to predict intangible duration or the amount of income flows. In this approach, the variations of the estimated remaining useful life of an intangible become less important as the estimated remaining useful life increases. Extremely short or long useful remaining values raise questions about the underlying reasons (external or internal to the library) for their existence. For instance, some organizational intellectual capital resources such as "user lists" may exhibit a short remaining useful life, while other intangibles such as copyrights have longer remaining useful lives. As Reilly and Schweihs (1998) indicate, from a life analysis perspective, no intangible resource can be assumed as being similar to another without a formal examination; this means that no "user list" is exactly the same as any other "user list," etc.

Problem definition and background information

The problem arising in reliability estimations can be described as follows (Kalbfleisch and Prentice, 2002). Let us assume that a collection of N identical and independent individuals, units, or items representing or associated to intangible resources are made available. After observing the life characteristics of the intangible resources/assets, the available data consist of a number of lifelength times (failures) and a number of truncated lifelength times (censoring). The latter is a result of lifetimes that have not reached the end point event of interest (remain unfailed) or have been removed prior to reaching it. At the end of the observation period, life data contain a set of lifetimes randomly intermixed with incomplete observations, in other words, multiply censored

Figure 6.1 Typical actions involved in the extraction of information from reliability data

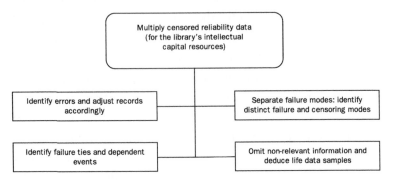

Source: Adopted from Kostagiolas, 2011.

reliability data. Multiply censored reliability data (Figure 6.1) may derive from a number of sources, such as library operational records, library user longevity, or personnel logs.

Life data for intangibles may include (Reilly and Schweihs, 1998):

- active intangible units (for example users, contracts, cooperations):

  - unique identification (user number, subscription number, contract, etc.);
  - initiation date (user registration, opening subscription account, etc.);
  - measurements associated with the intangible resource/ asset (average user transactions, renewals, delays, etc.);

- inactive, retired, terminated or failed intangible units:

  - unit identification;
  - life length (start and end date).

In many cases, however, the exact end or failure date is not known, even though it is certainly known that at some point after its initiation the intangible was active. In these cases censoring is observed. Omitting data of this nature, even though it significantly simplifies the analytical methods employed, reduces the available information. This is the case, for instance, when analyzing the survival of library contracts and their available number seems to be relatively small, with only a few of them being terminated before the predefined end date, presenting a failure time.

Before being submitted to the life analysis, data need to be cleared of errors, irrelevant information, failure ties, and dependent events. The distinct failure and censoring modes (different reasons or different definitions for failure) are identified and separated, while the observed times to failure or censoring are subjected to random deviations which are independent and identically distributed (iid) variables forming a probability distribution. Thereafter, probability distributions employed as models for the lifelength of events (organizational operations or services, information systems, etc.) are referred to as life distributions. The variable of interest is the lifetime of successful operation or the unchanged state of a specific intangible resource. The investigator attempts to estimate the survival function either through the data (nonparametric methods) or through fitting distributional models (parametric methods). Distributional modeling of reliability data is utilized with the purpose of extracting information from the multiply censored data by providing a more meaningful description and understanding of the underlying life characteristics of the failure event under study.

Basic probability functions for life analysis

A reliability analysis is determined through five time-dependent and mathematically equivalent probability functions, allowing probabilities to be assigned to the data. Several relations exist between these basic probability functions, making it possible to derive any of them if one is known (for example, Kostagiolas, 2000). All functions relate probabilities to the nonnegative variable (time) and are defined on the positive real axes, interval $[0, + \infty]$, unless stated otherwise. The five basic distribution functions, their meaning and relations are presented below.

- The probability density function (pdf), f(t) is defined as the probability of observing a failure within a small time interval $[t, t+\Delta t]$, as Δt tends to zero. The pdf is a nonnegative function, $f(t) \geq 0$ for all t, provides information about the proportion of failure events in any time interval (the frequency of failures in relation to time), and the area between the pdf and the time axes is defined to be unity,

$$\int_0^\infty f(t)\,dt = 1$$

- The cumulative distribution function (cdf), F(t), is defined as the integral of the pdf over the interval $[0, t]$ and represents the probability that a unit's lifetime does not exceed time t or the proportion of units whose lifetimes do not exceed time t.

$$F(t) = \int_0^\infty f(t)\,dt$$

- The reliability function, R(t), often also referred to as the survival function, is defined as the complement of the cdf,

$$R(t) = 1 - F(t),$$

and corresponds to the probability of a unit to survive up to time t, or the proportion of units that survive up to time t. The reliability function is a nonnegative strictly decreasing function defined as one for $t = 0$ (the probability of a unit surviving at least to time zero is one) and zero for $t = +\infty$ (the probability of a unit surviving to infinite time is zero).

- The hazard function (hf), $h(t)$, is defined as the conditional probability of an item to fail within the time interval $[t, t+\Delta t]$, having survived to time t and is derived through the following equation:

$$h(t) = f(t) \Big/ R(t)$$

The hazard function is a quantity of significant importance within the reliability theory and represents the instantaneous rate of failure at time t, given that the unit has survived up to time t. The hazard function is also referred to as the instantaneous failure rate, hazard rate, mortality rate, and force of mortality (Lawless, 1982), and measures failure-proneness as a function of age (Nelson, 1982). The hazard function may be increasing, decreasing, or constant through time. The representation of a life distribution through its hazard function is most commonly employed in reliability analysis.

- The cumulative hazard function (chf), $H(t)$, is defined as the integral of h(t) over the interval $[0,t]$:

$$H(t) = \int_0^1 h(u)\,du$$

The chf is a nonnegative strictly increasing function defined to be zero at $t = 0$ and $+\infty$.

The five probability functions are mathematically equivalent and if one of them is known, all five can be derived. The most important relations between the pdf, cdf, reliability, hazard, and chf functions are described, for example, in Lawless (1982). In fact, distributional modeling in reliability practice often starts with examining the form of the hazard function for the population under study. A constant hazard function, for instance, suggests an employment of the memoryless exponential distribution, implying that the future survival of a unit is not affected by past use. The constant hazard function, however, is rarely met and time-dependent alternative representations are usually required.

Nonparametric methods for estimating survival probabilities

Among the estimators proposed for the reliability (or survival) function in this section, we focus on nonparametric methods—that is, in cases where reliability is estimated directly from the data. The two prevalent nonparametric estimators employed are equally available, although due to their distinct formulation they result in distinct survival probabilities and are both approximations of the unique true sample survival function. Before proceeding any further, it would be useful to define the notation used: Let us assume that there is a multiply censored data set, consisting of N independent and identically distributed (iid) lifetimes. Let nf be the number of distinct times to failure denoted as T1,T2,. . .,Tnf. The data may be reordered by magnitude and written as:

$$0 < \tau_{01} \leq \ldots \leq \tau_{0e_0} < T_1 < \tau_{11} \leq \ldots \leq \tau_{1e_1} < T_2 < \ldots < T_j$$

$$< \tau_{j_i} \leq \ldots \leq \tau_{je_1} < \ldots < T_{nf} < \tau_{nf1} \leq \ldots \leq \tau_{nfe_{nf}},$$

where $T_0 = 0$ and $T_{nf+1} = \infty$. Strict inequality is assumed between failures and incomplete observations. Furthermore, let dj be the number of failures occurring at time Tj (j = 1, . . ., nf), with $d_0 = 0$—that is, there is no failure at time zero. Denote by e_j the number of right censored observations, that is, $\tau_{nf1}, \ldots, \tau_{nfe_{nf}}$ that fail in the interval $[T_j, T_{j+1})$ with j = 0, ..., nf. Let nj be the number of items "at risk of failure" comprising items with lifetimes higher or equal to Tj (j = 1, ..., nf),

$$n_j = \sum_{l=j}^{nf}(d_j + e_j) \Rightarrow n_0 = N \tag{6.1}$$

The density estimation procedures known as Kaplan-Meier (KM) and Cumulative-Hazard (CH) are briefly reviewed below.

A popular estimator of the survival function is the KM estimator, often referred to as the Product–Limit (PL) estimator, introduced by Kaplan and Meier (1958). The KM is a key quantity in several more complicated survival analysis models like the Proportional Hazards, Goodness Of Fit (GOF), and two-sample tests. The KM estimator itself is a step function which is defined through the product:

$$\hat{R}_{KM}(T_j) = \prod_{l=1}^{j} \frac{n_j - d_j}{n_j} \tag{6.2}$$

The CH procedure (Nelson, 1982) estimates the reliability function through a computation of the hazard and cumulative hazard functions (chf):

$$\hat{h}(T_j) = \frac{d_j}{n_j} \text{ and } \hat{H}(T_j) = \sum_{l=1}^{j}\hat{h}(T_j) \tag{6.3}$$

$$\hat{R}_{CH}(T_j) = \exp\left(-\hat{H}(T_j)\right) \tag{6.4}$$

When comparing the CH estimator with the KM, the following conclusions can be drawn (Kostagiolas and Bohoris, 2010): it results in higher survival probabilities; it has the same form as the KM estimator (that is, they are both step functions); it is at least as easy to calculate as the KM estimator; it is closely related to graphical assessment techniques (Cumulative Hazard Plots); and it tends only asymptotically to zero after the last event in the data. The KM estimator is defined to be zero if the last event happens to be a failure, leading to the rather extreme conclusion that no population failures are statistically possible beyond this point.

Parametric methods for estimating survival probabilities: The Weibull life model

The two-parameter Weibull distribution is an important lifetime model in reliability modeling. A review of the statistical methods of the Weibull distribution with censored data is provided in Dodson (2006). The reliability model is expressed through the Weibull distribution as follows: $R(t) = e^{-\left(\frac{t}{\eta}\right)^{\beta}}$ with β and η being the shape and scale Weibull parameters, respectively. The possible values of the two nonnegative Weibull parameters, and their combinations, provide great flexibility and therefore extensive applicability to statistical studies as well as to the reliability/maintenance practice. For example, when $\beta = 1$ the Weibull is simplified to an exponential distribution and when $\beta \in [3,4]$, it approximates the normal distribution. Another important attribute of the Weibull distribution is that it can serve as both a decreasing ($\beta < 1$) and increasing ($\beta > 1$) hazard function model. The Weibull model enjoys wide applicability thanks to its resilience and its ability to provide a good fit for many different types of reliability data.

Parametric reliability analysis methods are based on an estimation of the Weibull shape and scale parameters directly from the multiply censored data (Skinner et al., 2001). One popular method of parameter estimation with multiply censored data is the Maximum Likelihood Estimation (MLE) (for example, Dodson, 2006). This method is based on deducing the parameter values (say, $\hat{\beta}$ and $\hat{\eta}$) which maximize the log-likelihood function for a multiply censored data sample with nf failures and nc censoring: $\ln L = \sum_{i=1}^{nf} \ln f(t_i : \beta, \eta)$ $+ \sum_{i=1}^{nc} \ln R(t_i : \beta, \eta)$, where $f(t : \beta, \eta)$ and $R(t : \beta, \eta)$ are the pdf and the survival function of the Weibull distribution. The ML estimates the shape and scale parameters of the Weibull distribution, $\hat{\beta}$ and $\hat{\eta}$, respectively, and may be obtained by setting the partial derivatives of η and β in the equation above equal to zero,

$$\frac{\partial \ln L}{\partial \eta} = 0 \quad \Rightarrow \hat{\eta} = \left[\frac{\sum_{i=1}^{N} t_i^{\hat{\beta}}}{nf} \right]^{1/\hat{\beta}} \quad \text{and} \quad \frac{\partial \ln L}{\partial \beta} = 0$$

$$\Rightarrow \frac{1}{\hat{\beta}} + \frac{\sum_{i=1}^{nf} \ln t_i}{nf} - \frac{\sum_{i=1}^{N} t_i^{\hat{\beta}} \ln t_i}{\sum_{i=1}^{N} t_i^{\hat{\beta}}} = 0$$

Therefore, the MLE of the scale Weibull parameter ($\hat{\eta}$) can only be obtained after calculating $\hat{\beta}$. In the second nonlinear equation, however, the only unknown element is the Weibull shape parameter, which can be obtained through an appropriate convergence algorithm such as the Newton-Rampson method and the Van Wijngaarden-Dekker-Brent method (Press et al., 1986).

Illustrative example for library "user list" intangible resources

Let us assume that a subscription-based information service has been introduced in a library. The user subscriptions list is an extremely important intangible resource. The behavior of the users who accept it and are loyal to the library by renewing their subscription may further demonstrate the usefulness of the library's service and, in case there is a subscription fee, the library's potential revenue from subscriptions. Subscription cancelations or refusal to renew subscriptions would reduce the *remaining useful life* of this intangible asset, hence reducing the value of the subscription. On the other hand, the longevity of subscriptions would increase the value of this particular subscribed service for the library. Therefore, in this example,[1] it is significant to estimate the average life of subscriptions and predict the rate at which the users tend to cancel their subscriptions (namely, the "failure rate" for subscriptions).

Life analysis may be employed to study the time period for which a user remains subscribed to this particular service. The rate of the users who remain subscribed to the service on a long-term basis is, as noted before, an important issue for the library's management. Such estimation, however, should be based on predicting the rate at which the users renew or cancel their subscriptions, that is, the users' subscription failure rate. In this case, the actual failure rate and the reliability of the subscription can be estimated either from the data or by fitting a probability model such as the Weibull distribution, as presented above. Although such an analysis should include all available times to renewal or times to cancelation of all users, in the interest of simplicity, we will examine a sample of 21 subscribers. By knowing the start and end dates of their subscriptions, we can obtain a multiply censored data set, which includes times of cancelation/failure for each subscription and times of renewal/censoring. Table 6.1 includes all available lifetime data expressed in days, that is, N = 21 lifetimes out of which nf = 15 are failures and $n_c = \sum_{=0}^{nf} e_i = 6$ are censoring. For instance, examining the first three users, we actually observe that the first user of the sample has canceled their subscription after 69 days, the second after 176, while the third renewed their subscription after 195 days. Table 6.1 contains the basic sample quantities and the required computations for the estimation of the reliability function according to KM and CH, in columns five to seven. The computation of KM survival estimator is based on Equation 6.2 and is presented in column 11 of Table 6.1. The CH procedure involves an estimation of the hazard and the chf (Equation 6.3) and computations are presented in columns eight and nine, followed by an estimation of the survival function in column ten.

Thereafter, MLE is employed to estimate the parameters of the Weibull distribution for the multiply censored data of Table 6.1. The shape parameter was estimated to be $\hat{\beta} = 1.545$, while the scale parameter was estimated to be $\hat{\eta} = 648.784$. Reliability estimations are presented for all lifetimes (failures and censoring) in the last column of Table 6.1 and can be obtained from:

$$\hat{R}_o(t^*_{i=1,\dots,N}) = e^{-\left(\frac{1}{\hat{\eta}}\right)^{\hat{\beta}}} = e^{-\left(\frac{t}{648.784}\right)^{1.545}}$$

A visualization of the estimated Weibull distribution fit to the reliability data for user subscriptions may be obtained through a graphical GOF investigation provided in Figure 6.2. The graphs of Figure 6.2 result from three graphical Goodness Of Fit methods (GOF), the Q-Q, P-P, and S-P plots. The plotted points lie, for all plots, either below or above the solid line. In the Q-Q graph, the empirical cdf is again plotted in a straight line close to the solid line, suggesting that the shape of the distribution is adequate. On the other hand, the P-P method and its transformations (for example, S-P) result in plots of the empirical distribution against the hypothesized Weibull cdf with the time axis logarithmically transformed.

Table 6.1 Calculation of the basic sample quantities and the nonparametric reliability estimators for the multiply censored data set of Kostagiolas (2000)

Event number	Event time (days)	Failure number	Failure time (days)	Basic sample quantities			Hazard estimates	Cumulative Hazard function estimates	Nonparametric reliability estimates		Parametric Weibull reliability estimates
									CH	KM	
I	t_i^*	J	T_j	n_j	d_j	e_j	$\hat{h}_{CH}(T_j)$	$\hat{H}_{CH}(T_j)$	$\hat{R}_{CH}(T_j)$	$\hat{R}_{KM}(T_j)$	$\hat{R}_o(t_{I=1,\ldots,N}^*)$
1	69	1	69	21	1	0	0.048	0.048	0.954	0.952	0.969
2	176	2	176	20	1	1	0.050	0.098	0.907	0.905	0.875
3	−195	–	–	–	–	–	–	–	–	–	0.856
4	208	3	208	18	1	0	0.056	0.153	0.858	0.855	0.842
5	215	4	215	17	1	0	0.059	0.212	0.810	0.804	0.834
6	233	5	233	16	1	0	0.063	0.275	0.760	0.754	0.814
7	289	6	289	15	1	0	0.067	0.341	0.711	0.704	0.751
8	300	7	300	14	1	0	0.071	0.413	0.662	0.653	0.738
9	384	8	384	13	1	0	0.077	0.489	0.613	0.603	0.641
10	390	9	390	12	1	1	0.083	0.573	0.564	0.553	0.634
11	−393	–	–	–	–	–	–	–	–	–	0.631
12	441	10	441	10	1	0	0.100	0.673	0.510	0.498	0.577
13	453	11	453	9	1	0	0.111	0.784	0.457	0.442	0.563

14	567	12	567	8	1	2	0.125	0.909	0.403	0.387	0.444
15	-617	-	-	-	-	-	-	-	-	-	0.396
16	-718	-	-	-	-	-	-	-	-	-	0.311
17	719	13	719	5	1	0	0.200	1.109	0.330	0.310	0.310
18	783	14	783	4	1	0	0.250	1.359	0.257	0.232	0.263
19	900	15	900	3	1	2	0.333	1.692	0.184	0.155	0.191
20	-1000	-	-	-	-	-	-	-	-	-	0.142
21	-1022	-	-	-	-	-	-	-	-	-	0.133

* Negative lifetimes denote censored observations

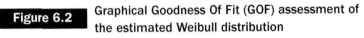

Figure 6.2 Graphical Goodness Of Fit (GOF) assessment of the estimated Weibull distribution

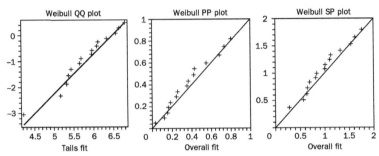

Source: Adapted from Kostagiolas, 2000.

In the P-P method, the logarithmic transformation of the abscissa results in deviations which are increasing in the middle of the plot. However, the transformation which defines the S-P graph does allow for differentiations in the shape parameter to appear against the estimated Weibull distribution. Figure 6.2 indicates a satisfactory agreement between the estimated Weibull model and the multiply censored data sample for user subscriptions (Kostagiolas, 2000).

The parametrically estimated Weibull distribution allows for extrapolation beyond available data. In fact, computing the Weibull parameters is the first step, while further conclusions regarding the longevity of library user subscriptions can be drawn through the employment of the conditional probability of the estimated Weibull model, namely the probability that a user will maintain their subscription for a certain length of time, given that they have already had a subscription for a given time period. The conditional probability is then obtained through the equation,

$$\hat{R}_o(T/t) = \frac{\hat{R}_o(T+t)}{\hat{R}_o(t)} = \frac{e^{-\left(\frac{T+t}{\hat{\eta}}\right)^{\hat{\beta}}}}{e^{-\left(\frac{t}{\hat{\eta}}\right)^{\hat{\beta}}}} = \frac{e^{-\left(\frac{T+t}{648.784}\right)^{1.545}}}{e^{-\left(\frac{t}{648.784}\right)^{1.545}}}$$

Table 6.2 contains the percentages of users who are expected to renew their subscriptions after a certain length of time (subscription age), namely the conditional probabilities of the estimated Weibull model for a wide range of combinations of subscription ages (first column in Table 6.2) and time periods, that is, 0 (60) 600 days as shown in the second row of Table 6.2. For instance, we argue that after about six months of subscription, the percentage of users that we expect to renew their subscription for another six months is about 66.86 per cent.

Applications of library intangible resource reliability analysis

The life analysis for library operations and services constitutes an important aspect for the management of intellectual capital resources, not yet investigated sufficiently in the literature. The survival analysis applications of intellectual capital include methods for comparing parametrically or nonparametrically the reliability of different intangibles (two-sample or multiple-sample problem), demonstrating that a unit meets the specified reliability criteria, making predictions about reliability performance during an intangible's entire lifecycle (or specific parts of its lifecycle such as the service life, economical life, legal life, technological life, functional life), modeling the underlying mechanisms that produce failures and thus developing specific intangible resource maintenance strategies, using reports to communicate intangible reliability performance effectively to library management, etc. The development of preventive maintenance and repair plans needs to be addressed in the future in order to reduce or avoid a decrease in the reliability

Table 6.2 Percentages of the users expected to renew their subscription based on conditional probabilities of the estimated Weibull distribution

Percentage (%) of users expected to renew their subscription after a given period of time (in days)

Subscription age (days)	0	60	120	180	240	300	360	420	480	540	600
0	100.00	97.50	92.89	87.11	80.64	73.81	66.86	60.00	53.38	47.09	41.22
60	97.50	92.89	87.11	80.64	73.81	66.86	60.00	53.38	47.09	41.22	35.81
120	92.89	87.11	80.64	73.81	66.86	60.00	53.38	47.09	41.22	35.81	30.89
180	87.11	80.64	73.81	66.86	60.00	53.38	47.09	41.22	35.81	30.89	26.47
240	80.64	73.81	66.86	60.00	53.38	47.09	41.22	35.81	30.89	26.47	22.53
300	73.81	66.86	60.00	53.38	47.09	41.22	35.81	30.89	26.47	22.53	19.05
360	66.86	60.00	53.38	47.09	41.22	35.81	30.89	26.47	22.53	19.05	16.01
420	60.00	53.38	47.09	41.22	35.81	30.89	26.47	22.53	19.05	16.01	13.37
480	53.38	47.09	41.22	35.81	30.89	26.47	22.53	19.05	16.01	13.37	11.11
540	47.09	41.22	35.81	30.89	26.47	22.53	19.05	16.01	13.37	11.11	9.17
600	41.22	35.81	30.89	26.47	22.53	19.05	16.01	13.37	11.11	9.17	7.53

of intellectual capital resources. For that purpose, specific risk factors and hazards need to be identified, categorized, and associated with intellectual capital library resources.

All the above-mentioned facts call for the development of a specific subsection of the library's intellectual capital management theoretical framework which needs to be systematically constructed through the wide array of survival analysis methods that are available in the literature. Reliability analysis methods from biomedical studies, engineering, and manufacturing may be further discussed or modified in order to comprise the special requirements of this field. Indicatively, these methods may include the investigation of theoretical issues for defining failure modes in a variety of library situations and for different intangible resources/assets, maintenance and repair planning, analysis of competing failure modes with reliability block diagrams, parametric (for example the Weibull models) or nonparametric methods to analyze events that may or may not be dependent, or may or may not be identically distributed due to intangible maintenance actions, GOF methods for assessing reliability modeling, extrapolation methods to predict reliability beyond the observed failure times and throughout the whole lifecycle period, investigation of reliability confidence bounds, testing scenarios, etc.

For human capital resources, the study of human reliability in the library sector is related to the investigation of human factors including human safety risks, ergonomics, personnel age, physical and mental health, attitude, errors and mistakes, etc. that have an effect on the library's reliability. A wide number of theoretical methods and techniques have been made available as regards human reliability and can be employed for human capital library intangible resources. For organizational capital resources, conventional and digital library operations, systems, and services may be assessed in terms of their reliability characteristics. For example, remote services, digital repositories, and other automation systems can be assessed in terms of the different client errors (such as bad request, unauthorized, forbidden, not found), server error (internal server error, not implemented, bad gateway, service unavailable, gateway timeout), or other error log files. Similarly, user-oriented organizational intellectual capital resources such as user lists, and user subscriptions can also be assessed in terms of their lifecycle survival characteristics. Finally, life analysis can be applied to relational intangible resources, such as contracts, relation status among different libraries or between libraries and other organizations or businesses. The effect of the reliability variations for different intangibles is not equally important and hence survival analysis can be applied only to those with the highest reliability priority. Intellectual capital reliability indications may provide information to the management as regards maintenance and renewal policies and actions.

A further holistic approach towards reliability may aim at developing best practices in an effective and applicable manner so as to provide highly reliable operations, systems, and services. Such an approach may include a reliability plan which will contain a number of activities performed at the right time in order to achieve and maintain the required and predefined reliability level. Such a plan should be an important organizational intangible asset in itself and its implementation should incorporate processes and organizational and cultural aspects. Furthermore, it should be supported by the top management and be simple to use in everyday practices by the library's staff. Personnel training and top management commitment are very important for making the right decisions as regards the services and operations that reliability modeling will focus on, how data will be extracted and analyzed, what the distributional models are that can fit to the available data in order to express the underlying mechanisms, etc.

Summary

As competition becomes global and constantly increases, and as resources become scarce, the management of library intellectual capital should include reliability performance information. Gradually, many pieces of the library service quality puzzle have fallen into place and as a result the international literature has been flooded with case studies and theoretical quality paradigms. Moreover, information technologies have been made widely available and have been employed by the majority of libraries all over the world, homogenizing and standardizing their operations and services. However, external and internal issues have an effect on the reliability characteristics of intangibles (such as the remaining useful life) throughout their lifecycle. Situations where reliability analysis can be used in library intellectual capital management may include intangibles of all three categories (human, organizational, and relational) such as user behavior, conventional library operations and services, digital library operations and services, relations, and contracts.

Note

1. This example has been presented in Kostagiolas (2011) and similar examples have been presented in *www.weibull.com/ hotwire/issue14/hottopics14.htm* and for grouped survival data in Reilly et al. (1999).

7

Putting it all together: summary and final thoughts for further research

Abstract: Throughout this book an attempt has been made to present and interrelate the elements of library intellectual capital management as a system, attempting to discuss the most appropriate methods and techniques for each intellectual capital aspect: identification and categorization, prioritization, measurement and reporting, financial valuation, and lifecycle analysis. The purpose of this concluding chapter is twofold: firstly, to summarize the interrelations of the different methods and techniques for library intellectual capital, and secondly, to provide the author's thoughts for further research on this innovative and exciting area of library management.

Key words: system analysis, innovation, entrepreneurship, environmental trends.

A systems perspective for library intellectual capital management

Intellectual capital resources for the majority of organizations and enterprises constitute just an additional—though very important—issue to be analyzed and dealt with. Especially during the past 20 years, the study of intellectual capital management has been linked with several scientific fields and thus many interrelated concepts, methods, and techniques have been derived from different disciplines and different viewpoints. Intellectual capital and libraries, however, are closely interrelated in our experiences and minds. Library and information professionals, as noted in Chapter 2, throughout their long history have consciously or unconsciously been deeply involved in the management of library intellectual capital resources. Libraries contain and accumulate human memory, and library professionals are the gatekeepers of our past. This is an invaluable and unique intangible heritage which is traditionally managed by librarians and information professionals, and is kept and organized within libraries in order to be available for future generations.

The methods and techniques presented in this book within each distinct chapter are related to each other and should be seen as a management continuum. As stated in the "Introduction of the Revised Edition" of Drucker (2008), one should ". . . understand and apply the subject of management as an organic whole and not merely as a set of isolated elements." Figure 7.1 provides a system view of library intellectual capital management as a whole, connecting all distinct elements presented in this book. Library intellectual capital environmental tradition and trends were analyzed in Chapters 1 and 2, providing a political, economical, social, technological, and legal conceptual framework on which the library's management system is based and developed. Furthermore, methods and techniques are adjusted in terms of their applicability in libraries from a pool of newly developed and either general or industry-specific perspectives. These adjusted or newly developed methods include identification and categorization approaches (Chapter 3), measuring and hierarchy frameworks (Chapter 4), financial valuation and reporting techniques (Chapter 5), and intangible life analysis methods (Chapter 6). All these aspects constitute the

Figure 7.1 A systems view for library intellectual capital management

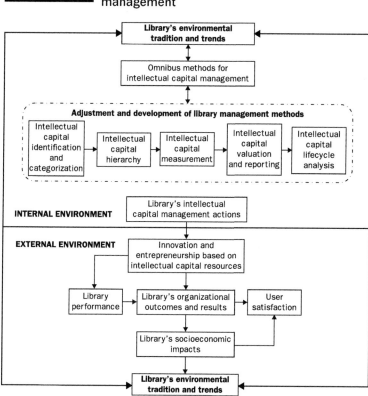

Source: Modified from Drucker, 2008.

continuum of library intellectual capital management which is being put in practice to support library management decisions and actions as regards its internal environment. One should, however, apply all these methods with caution according to their specifications and their intended use. For instance, as we have already mentioned, it is difficult if not impossible to estimate accurately the financial value of a unique historic old library collection, and it is difficult if not impossible to estimate the value created by a public library when a child's life is saved by a children's disease prevention program!

Despite their uniqueness, libraries are organizations with resources that need to be managed and they cannot avoid pressure from their external environment (as shown in the lower part of Figure 7.1) including, in some cases, fierce socioeconomic realities. It is only logical that people all over the world are massively concerned with the economic depression and the impact that it might have on their quality of life, their communities, their children's futures, their retirement, and society as a whole (Rooney-Browne, 2008). Under these circumstances, library financing may no longer be taken for granted, while the international economic reality might include several important drawbacks for libraries, such as financial resource shortage and lack of staff. Libraries now need, more than ever, to prove their value and enhance their entrepreneurship through the exploitation of their tangible and intangible resources (Kostagiolas et al., 2011):

> Libraries stand at a crossroad of opportunity brought about by the confluence of economic and social challenges that the economic recession has caused, while—in parallel—the developments in information technologies provide a wider range of services and more channels of access to them.

In a similar manner, Davis (2006) suggests switching from high-cost systemic library reforms and investments to a framework of fully exploring the potential of the librarian's creative energies and encouraging library innovation, inclusion, and participation. In order to increase social value and overall socioeconomic impact, the management of libraries should be proactive and able to foresee, when possible, the changing social and economic needs of communities. Socioeconomic development largely depends upon an active, socially cohesive, and well-informed population that has access to information sources.

Furthermore, innovative and proactive intellectual capital management might urge libraries to internalize intangible resources from their external environment in order to develop value added services further. Resources of this nature may include community information on local organizations, the government and services of all kinds, local events, places to visit, leisure and sporting venues, business information that builds business relations, legal information on national–international laws and regulations, specialized literature, genealogical searches, technical standards, reports, personalized services tailored to the needs of individuals or groups, training courses on the use of technology and website hosting and management, especially designed display areas for artists, career information, fundraising activities, etc. All these services contain intellectual capital resources related to the library's (proactive) role which increases the ability of libraries to escape from perplexities and find ways to relax fiscal constraints in order to remain sustainable and look for alternative funding. According to the president of the ALA,[1] during tough economic times, people turn to libraries for free resources, from computers to books, DVDs, and CDs, for help with job hunting or health information. It is not strange that library use is increasing in times of economic depression, when more people are turning to libraries for information, training, literacy programs, computer skills development, etc., taking advantage of the available free intellectual resources (for example, Seavey, 2003; ALA, 2007; ALA, 2008a; ALA, 2008b; Sheffer, 2008; Goulding, 2009; Mostad-Jensen, 2009). Incorporating intellectual capital into total value estimations and contributions may come to rescue libraries in the era of worldwide economic instability.

Thoughts for future research

It seems very probable that the scientific dialog and the interdisciplinary approaches to library intellectual capital management can make an important contribution to the future development of libraries. The theoretical ideas and approaches that have been discussed in this book all support the view that, if managed properly, library intellectual capital can improve in sustainability, efficiency, effectiveness, productivity, and quality. It is deemed almost certain that the presence of intangible assets increases the value of assets presented in the library's balance sheet. In fact, a number of examples were presented for investments in intellectual capital which, within the right framework, can provide a competitive advantage for the library or prove the library's value to stakeholders. At the international level, the scientific dialog on intellectual capital management has started and will hopefully be developed further as a result of the increasing socioeconomic pressures experienced by libraries.

Exciting and innovative research pathways through the employment of quantitative, qualitative, and mixed methods can be identified as regards library intellectual capital management. The more one ventures into relevant matters, the more innovative practical and theoretical issues and questions are acknowledged. Moreover, the very nature of intellectual capital management suggests that the same research question can be examined from a number of perspectives including interdisciplinary or mono-disciplinary aspects. A list of topics is presented below, as food for thought and a source of inspiration for further advances on the subject:

■ a history of intellectual capital contributions to the field of library and information science;

- library directors' perceptions of library intellectual capital management;
- library staff skills for intellectual capital management;
- information technologies and systems for capturing and managing intellectual capital resources;
- a comprehensive taxonomy of library intellectual capital assets/resources;
- intangible metrics, measurement methods and intangible hierarchy identification for different types of libraries;
- the impact and value of libraries to the intellectual capital of the systems they belong to, for example, a public library and its community, an academic library and the academic environment, a hospital library and the hospital;
- contribution of the library's intellectual capital resources to sustainability, innovation, co-opetition dynamics, performance, and quality;
- financial valuation methods and approaches to library intellectual capital resources;
- library reporting frameworks based on intellectual capital assets/resources;
- nonparametric and parametric modeling for assumptions on the survival characteristics of intellectual capital resources for an individual library or comparing different resources or distinct libraries;
- comprehension and modeling associations between human, structural, and relational intellectual capital resources with factors affecting operations, services, and decision making within the library's organizational structure;
- user preferences and attitudes towards library intellectual capital resources;

- convergence based on sharing and exchanging intellectual capital resources among memory organizations and institutions such as libraries, museums, and archives;
- Library 2.0 intellectual capital resources;
- library goodwill as an intellectual capital resource.

As noted before, this book on library intellectual capital management aims at increasing the overall awareness and knowledge of the subject by creating a body of relevant material as a foundation for further practical and theoretical intellectual pursuits. Certainly, this book did not attempt to address all relevant concerns, since this would be an impossible task.

Note

1. *www.ala.org/ala/issuesadvocacy/advocacy/advocacyuniversity/toolkit/index.cfm*

References

Aabo, S. (2009) "Libraries and return on investment (ROI): a meta-analysis," *New Library World*, 110(7/8): 311–24.

ALA (2007) "The state of America's libraries," American Library Association's Public Information Office, Washington, available at *www.ala.org/ala/newspresscenter/ mediapresscenter/presskits/2008statereport/2008stateh ome.cfm*.

ALA (2008a) "Slow economy fuels surge in library visits," Press Release, August 26, available at *www.ala.org/ala/ newspresscenter/news/pressreleases2008/august2008/ RettigEconomy.cfm*.

ALA (2008b) "Libraries and the economy," Advocacy Toolkit, available at *www.ala.org/ala/issuesadvocacy/advocacy/ advocacyuniversity/toolkit/talkingpoints/economy.cfm*.

Andreou, A.N., Green, A., and Stankosky, M. (2007) "A framework of intangible valuation areas and antecedents," *Journal of Intellectual Capital*, 8(1): 52–75.

Andriessen, D. (2004) *Making Sense of Intellectual Capital: Designing a Method for the Valuation of Intangibles*, Oxford: Elsevier Butterworth-Heinemann.

Andriessen, D. (2005) "Implementing the KPMG Value Explorer: critical success factors for applying IC measurement tools," *Journal of Intellectual Capital*, 6(4): 474–88.

Anfruns, J. (2009) "The role of International Council of Museums for the safeguarding of intangible heritage and museums' development of intangible assets," *World*

Conference on Intellectual Capital for Communities in the Knowledge Economy (IC5), Paris, France, available at *http://info.worldbank.org/etools/docs/library/251715/ Anfruns%20Intangible%20heritage%20Final.pdf*.

Anttiroiko, A.-V. and Savolainen, R. (2007) "New premises of public library strategies in the Age of Globalization," in Edward D. Garten, Delmus E. Williams, James M. Nyce, and Sanna Talja (eds) *Advances in Library Administration and Organization*, (25): 61–81.

Ark, B. (2002) "Understanding productivity and income differentials among OECD countries: a survey," *The Review of Economics Performance and Social Progress*, 69–72, available at *www.csls.ca/repsp/2/bartvanark.pdf*.

Asonitis, St. and Kostagiolas, P. (2010) "An analytic hierarchy approach for intellectual capital: evidence for the Greek central public libraries," *Library Management*, 31(3): 145–61.

Banou, C. and Kostagiolas, P.A. (2007) "Managing expectations for open access in Greece: perceptions from the publishers and academic libraries, ELPUB2007, openness in digital publishing: awareness, discovery and access," Leslie Chan and Bob Martens (eds), *Proceedings of the 11th International Conference on Electronic Publishing*, Vienna, Austria, pp. 229–38, available at *http://elpub.scix. net/cgi-bin/works/Show?121_elpub2007*.

Barnes, M., Clayborne, J., and Palmer, S.S. (2005) "Book pricing: publisher, vendor, and library perspectives," *Collection Building*, 24(3): 87–91.

Barron, D.D. (1995) "Staffing rural public libraries: the need to invest in intellectual capital," *Library Trends*, 44(1): 77–87.

Baruch, L. (2001) *Intangibles: Measurement, Management and Reporting*, Washington, DC: Brookings Institution Press.

Baum, G., Ittner, C.D., Larcker, D.F., Low, J., Siesfeld, T., and Malone, M.S. (2000) "Introducing the new value creation index," New York: Forbes.

Bénaud, C.-L. and Bordeianu, S. (1999) "Outsourcing in academic libraries: a selective bibliography," *Reference Services Review*, 27(1): 78–89.

Bengtsson, M., Eriksson, J., and Wincent, J. (2010) "Co-opetition dynamics—an outline for further inquiry," *Journal of Global Competitiveness*, 20(2): 194–214.

Bonfour, A. (2003) "The IC-dVAL approach," *Journal of Intellectual Capital*, 4(3): 396–412.

Bontis, N. (2000) "Assessing knowledge assets: a review of the models used to measure intellectual capital, closing keynote presentation," *KM World*, September 15, Santa Clara, California.

Bontis, N. (2002) *World Congress on Intellectual Capital Reading*, Boston: Butterworth-Heinemann.

Bontis, N. (2004) "National Intellectual Capital Index: A United Nations initiative for the Arab region," *Journal of Intellectual Capital*, 5(1): 13–39.

Bouteiller, C. (2000) "The evaluation of intangibles: advocating of an option based approach," presented at Alternative Perspectives of Finance and Accounting Conference, Hamburg, August 4–6.

Brannstrom, D. and Giuliani, M. (2009) "Accounting for intellectual capital: a comparative analysis," *VINE: The Journal of Information and Knowledge Management Systems*, 39(1): 68–79.

British Library (2004) *Measuring our value*, available at *www.bl.uk/pdf/measuring.pdf*.

Broady-Preston, J. and Felice, J. (2006) "Customers, relationships and libraries: University of Malta—a case study," *Aslib Proceedings: New Information Perspectives*, 58(6): 525–36.

Broady-Preston, J. and Lobo, A. (2011) "Measuring the quality, value and impact of academic libraries: the role of external standards," *Performance Measurement and Metrics*, 12(2): 122–35.

Brooking, A. (1996) *Intellectual Capital: Core Assets for the Third Millennium Enterprise*, London: Thomson Business Press.

Brophy, P. (2008) "Telling the story: qualitative approaches to measuring the performance of emerging library services," *Performance Library and Metrics*, 9(1): 7–17.

Brown, D.J. (2010) "Repositories and journals: are they in conflict? A literature review of relevant literature," *Aslib Proceedings: New Information Perspectives*, 62(2): 112–43.

Bryson, J. (2001) "Measuring the performance of libraries in the knowledge economy and society," *Australian Academic & Research Libraries*, 32(4), available at *http://alia.org. au/publishing/aarl/32.4/full.text/bryson.html*.

Bueno, E., Merino, C., and Salmador, M.P. (2003) "Towards a model of intellectual capital in public administrations," presented at 3rd International Conference of Iberoamerican Academy of Management, December 7–10, Sao Paulo.

Burke, M.E. (2011) "Knowledge sharing in emerging economies," *Library Review*, 60(1): 5–14.

Canibano, L., Sanchez, P., Garcia-Ayuso, M., Chaminade, C., Olea, M., and Escobar, C.G. (1999) "Measuring intangibles: discussion of selected indicators. Spanish case study," presented to The International Symposium: Measuring and Reporting Intellectual Capital: Experience, Issues, and Prospects, OECD, Amsterdam, available at *www.oecd.org/dsti/sti/industry/indcompt/act/Ams-conf/ symposium*.

Childs, P. (2006) "Sssh! The quiet revolution," *New Library World*, 107(1222/1223): 149–56.

Choong, K.K. (2008) "Intellectual capital: definitions, categorization and reporting models," *Journal of Intellectual Capital*, 9(4): 609–38.

Choudhary, P.K., Shokeen, A., and Tripathi, R. (2011) "Sustaining public library system and services through marketing business resources to small entrepreneurs, Proceedings of 56th National Conference of Indian Library Association on "Public Libraries of the Future: Opportunities and Challenges," available at *http://dspace.jgu.edu.in:8080/dspace/bitstream/123456789/181/1/Sustaining%20 Public%20Library%20System%20%26%20Services% 20through%20Marketing%20Business%20Resources%20 to%20Small%20Entrepreneurs%2022.pdf*.

Chowdhury, G., Poulter, A., and McMenemy, D. (2006) "At the sharp end, Public Library 2.0. Towards a new mission for public libraries as a 'network of community knowledge'," *Online Information Review*, 30 (4): 454–60.

Chung, H-K. (2007) "Measuring the economic value of special libraries," *Bottom Line: Managing Library Finances*, 20(1): 30–44.

Cohen, J.A. (2005) *Intangible Assets: Valuation and Economic Benefits*, Hoboken, NJ: John Wiley & Sons, Inc.

Corrall, S. and Sriborisutsakul, S. (2010) "Evaluating intellectual assets in university libraries: a multi-site case study from Thailand," in S. Chu, W. Ritter, and S. Hawamdeh (eds), *Managing Knowledge for Global and Collaborative Innovations, Series on Innovation and Knowledge Management*, 8: 269–82.

Cribb, G. (2005) "Human resource development: impacting on all four perspectives of the Balanced Scoreboard," presented in World Library and Information Congress: 71st IFLA General Conference and Council ("Libraries—A voyage of discovery"), Oslo, August 14–28, available at: *http://archive.ifla.org/IV/ifla71/papers/075e-Cribb.pdf*.

Dakers, H. (1998) "Intellectual Capital: auditing the people assets," *INSPEL*, 32(4): 234–42.

Davis, D.M. (2007) "Library networks, cooperatives and consortia: a national survey," American Library Association, available at *www.ala.org/ala/research/librarystats/cooperatives/lncc/Final%20report.pdf*.

Davis, R. (2006) "CALIMERA: mobilizing local cultural institutions for citizens," *New Library World*, 107(1/2): 57–72.

Deakin, S. and Michie, J. (1997) "The theory and practice of contacting," presented in Simon Deakin and Jonathan Michie (eds), *Contracts, Co-operation, and Competition, Studies in Economics, Management and Law*, Oxford: Oxford University Press.

Dhillon, V. (2011) "Knowledge dispersion index for measuring intellectual capital," available at *http://arxiv.org/PS_cache/arxiv/pdf/1106/1106.2601v1.pdf*.

DMSTI (2003) "Intellectual capital statements—the new guideline," Copenhagen, Denmark, Danish Ministry of Science, Technology and Innovation.

Dodson, B. (2006) *The Weibull Analysis Handbook*, Milwaukee, WI: ASQ, Quality Press.

Drucker, P. (2008) *Management* (rev. edn), New York: Harper & Row.

Edvinsson, L. (2002) *Corporate Longitude*, Pearson Education, BookHouse Publishing, available at *www.corporatelongitude.com*.

Edvinsson, L. and Malone, M.S. (1997) *Intellectual Capital: Realizing Your Company's True Value by Finding Its Hidden Brainpower*, New York: Harper Business.

Enser, P. (2001) "On continuity, culture, competition—cooperation and convergence too," *New Library World*, 102(1170/1171): 423–8.

Fernandez-Molina, J.C. and Guimaraes, J.A.C. (2009) "The

WIPO development agenda and the contribution of the international library community," *The Electronic Library*, 27(6): 1010–25.

Fidel, R. (2008) "Are we there yet? Mixed methods research in library and information science," *Library & Information Science Research*, 30: 265–72.

Flamholtz, E. (1985) *Human Resource Accounting and Effective Organizational Control: Theory and Practice*, Hoboken, NJ: Jossey Bass.

Gallego, I. and Rodríguez, L. (2005) "Situation of intangible assets in Spanish firms: an empirical analysis," *Journal of Intellectual Capital*, 6(1): 105–26.

Garnes, K. (2007) "Library in the digital age: experiences and challenges from the university of Bergen library, Norway," available at *https://bora.uib.no/bitstream/ 1956/2459/1/LUCRARIBIBLIO_2007_Garnes.pdf*.

Germano, M. (2011) "The library value deficit," *Bottom Line: Managing Library Finances*, 24(2): 100–6.

Google (2010) Google books library project (Internet), available at *http://books.google.com/googlebooks/library. html*.

Goulding, A. (2009) "Credit crunch: the impact on libraries," *Journal of Information and Library Science*, 41(3), available at *http://lis.sagepub.com/cgi/reprint/41/1/3*.

Grasenick, K. and Low, J. (2004) "Shaken, not stirred. Defining and connecting indicators for the measurement and valuation of intangibles," *Journal of Intellectual Capital*, 5(2): 268–81.

Green, A. and Ryan, J. (2005) "A framework of intangible valuation areas," *Journal of Intellectual Capital*, 6(1): 43–52.

Grzeschik, K. (2010) "Return on investment (ROI) in German libraries: the Berlin School of Library and Information Science and the University Library at the

Humboldt University, Berlin—a case study," *Bottom Line: Managing Library Finances*, 23(4): 141–201.

Hand, J. and Lev, B. (2003) *Intangible Assets*, New York, NY: Oxford University Press.

Harris, M. (2006) "Technology, innovation and post-bureaucracy: the case of the British Library," *Journal of Organizational Change Management*, 19(1): 80–92.

Harris, P. (2002) "European challenge: developing global organizations," *European Business Review*, 4(6), 416–25.

Holt, G. (2007) "Communicating the value of your libraries," *Bottom Line: Managing Library Finances*, 20(3): 119–24.

Hood, D. and Henderson, K. (2005) "Branding in the United Kingdom public library service," *New Library World*, 106(1208/1209): 16–28.

Hsieh, L.-F., Chin, J.-B., and Wu, M.-C. (2006) "Performance evaluation for university electronic libraries in Taiwan," *The Electronic Library*, 24(2): 212–24.

Ishizaka, A. (2004) "Advantages of clusters and pivots in AHP," in *Proceedings of the 15th Mini-Euro Conference*, Coimbra, Portugal.

Ishizaka, A. and Lusti, M. (2006) "How to derive priorities in AHP: a comparative study," *Central European Journal of Operational Research*, 14(4): 387–400.

ISO 11620:1998 (1998) *Information and Documentation—Library Performance Indicators*, Geneva: International Organization for Standardization.

ISO/TR 20983:2003 (2003) *Information and Documentation—Performance Indicators for Electronic Library Services*, Geneva: International Organization for Standardization.

Jefcoate, G. (2006) "Gabriel: gateway to Europe's national libraries," *Program: Electronic Library and Information Systems*, 40(4): 325–33.

Johansson, U., Koga, C., Almqvist, R., and Skoog, M. (2009) "Implementing intellectual assets-based management guidelines," *Journal of Intellectual Capital*, 10(4): 520–38.

Jones, N., Meadow, C., and Sicilia, M.-A. (2009) "Measuring intellectual capital in higher education," *Journal of Information & Knowledge Management*, 8(2): 113–36.

Kalbfleisch, J.D. and Prentice, R.L. (2002) *The Statistical Analysis of Failure Time Data*, New York: Wiley-InterScience.

Kannan, G. and Aulbur, W.G. (2004) "Intellectual capital: measurement effectiveness," *Journal of Intellectual Capital*, 5(3): 389–413.

Kaplan, E.L. and Meier, P. (1958) "Nonparametric estimation from incomplete observations," *Journal of the American Statistical Association*, 53: 457–81.

Kaplan, R.S. and Norton, D.P. (1996) *The Balanced Scorecard: Translating Strategy Into Action*, Boston, MA: Harvard Business School Press.

Kaplan, R.S. and Norton, D.P. (1992) "The balanced scorecard measures that drive performance," *Harvard Business Review*, 71–9.

Kaplan, R.S. and Norton, D.P. (2001) "Transforming the balanced scorecard from performance measurement to strategic management: Part 1," *Accounting Horizons*, 15(1): 75–85.

Katsirikou, A. (2004) "Libraries' future through co-operations," *Libraries and Information*, 17: 19–21.

Kaufmann, L. and Schneider, Y. (2004) "Intangibles: a synthesis of current research," *Journal of Intellectual Capital*, 5(3): 366–88.

Kelly, J.C. (2007) "Creating an institutional repository at a challenged institution," *OCLC Systems & Services: International Digital Library Perspectives*, 23(2): 142–7.

Koening, M. (1997) "Intellectual capital and how to leverage it," *Bottom Line: Managing Library Finances*, 10(3): 112–18.

Kostagiolas, P.A. (2000) *The Goodness of Fit Problem with Industrial Reliability Data*, Ph.D. thesis, University of Birmingham, UK.

Kostagiolas, P.A. (2011) "Theory, methods and applications of reliability analysis in library management," *Proceedings of 3rd International Conference on Qualitative and Quantitative Methods in Libraries*, Athens, Greece.

Kostagiolas, P.A. and Asonitis, St. (2007) "The significance of the valuation of intangible assets for the social economy," *Pan-Hellenic Conference of the New Public Management—Social Responsibility and Citizen Society*, Department of Business Management, Aegean University, June, Chios, Greece.

Kostagiolas, P.A. and Asonitis, St. (2008) "Utilizing intangible assets in the Worlds of Production," *The International Journal of Knowledge, Culture and Change Management*, 8(2): 1–8.

Kostagiolas, P.A. and Asonitis, St. (2009) "Intangible assets for the academic libraries: definitions, categorization and an exploration of management issues," *Library Management*, 30(6/7): 419–29.

Kostagiolas, P.A. and Asonitis, St. (2011) "Managing intellectual capital in libraries and information services," *Advances in Librarianship*, 33: 31–50.

Kostagiolas, P.A. and Bohoris, G.A. (2010) "Information services for supporting quality and safety management," in N. Gulpinar and J.-R. Cordoba-Pachon (eds), *Proceedings of OR52 Conference: Stream on Information Systems and Knowledge Management*, Royal Holloway, School of Management, University of London, 84–8, Operation Research Society, UK.

Kostagiolas, P.A., Margiola, A., and Avramidou, A. (2011) "A library management response model against the economic crisis: The case of public libraries in Greece," *Library Review*, 60(6): 486–500.

Krishnamurthy, M. (2008) "Open access, open source and digital libraries: A current trend in university libraries around the world," *Program: Electronic Library and Information Systems*, 42(1): 48–54.

Kyrillidou, M. (2010a) "Library value may be proven, if not self-evident," *Research Library Issues: A Bimonthly Report from ARL, CNI, and SPARC*, no. 271 (August 2010), 1–3, available at *www.arl.org/resources/pubs/rli/ archive/rli271.shtml*.

Kyrillidou, M. (2010b) "The ARL Library Scorecard Pilot: Using the Balanced Scorecard in Research Libraries," *Research Library Issues: A Bimonthly Report from ARL, CNI, and SPARC*, no. 271 (August 2010), 36–40, available at *www.arl.org/resources/pubs/rli/archive/rli271.shtml*.

Lam, K. and Zhao, X. (1998) "An application of quality function deployment to improve the quality of teaching," *International Journal of Quality & Reliability Management*, 15(4): 389–413.

Lawless, J.F. (1982) *Statistical Methods and Models for Lifetime Data*, New York: John Wiley and Sons.

Lerner, F. (2001) *The Story of Libraries: From the Invention of Writing to the Computer Age*, New York: Continuum.

Lev, B. (1999) *Seeing is Believing—A Better Approach To Estimating Knowledge Capital*, CFO magazine.

Lev, B. (2001) *Intangibles: Management, Measurement and Reporting*, Washington, DC: The Brookings Institution.

Liebowitz, J. and Suen, Ch.Y. (2000) "Developing knowledge management metrics for measuring intellectual capital," *Journal of Intellectual Capital*, 1(1): 54–67.

Livonen, M. and Huotari, M. (2007) "The university library's intellectual capital," *Advances in Library Administration and Organization*, 25: 83–96.

Lucier, R.E. (2003) "Librarians and publishers as collaborators and competitors, e-content," *EDUCAUSE Review*, pp. 10–11, available at *http://net.educause.edu/ir/library/pdf/erm0326.pdf*.

Mahesh, G. and Mittal, R. (2009) "Digital content creation and copyright issues," *Electronic Library*, 27(4): 676–83.

Manez, J.A., Rochina, M.E., and Sanchis, J.A. (2008) "Using survival models with individual data," in E. Congregado (ed.), *Measuring Entrepreneurship: Building a Statistical System*, New York: Springer.

Marcum, J.W. (2008) "Sustainable library imperative partnering for innovation and sustainability," *Bottom Line: Managing Library Finances*, 21(3): 82–4.

Mard, M.J., Hitchner, J.R., and Hyden, S.D. (2007) *Valuation for Financial Reporting: Fair Value, Measurements and Reporting, Intangible Assets, Goodwill and Impairment*, Hoboken, NJ: John Wiley & Sons.

Materska, K. (2004) "Librarians in the knowledge age," *New Library World*, 105(1198/1999): 142–8.

McCallum, I. and Quinn, S. (2004) "Valuing libraries," *The Australian Library Journal*, 53(1): 55–70.

McCutcheon, G. (2008) "EVVICAE, a valuation model for intellectual asset-rich businesses," *Measuring Business Excellence*, 12(2): 79–96.

McPherson, P. and Pike, S. (2001) "Accounting, empirical measurement and intellectual capital," *Journal of Intellectual Capital*, 2(3): 246–60.

MERITUM (2002) *MERITUM Guidelines for Managing & Reporting on Intangibles*, Measuring Intangibles to

Understand and Improve Innovation Management— MERITUM, Madrid, Spain.

Milost, F. (2007) "A dynamic monetary model for evaluating employees," *Journal of Intellectual Capital*, 8(1): 124–38.

Missingham, R. (2005) "Libraries and economic value: a review of recent studies," *Performance Measurements and Metrics*, 6(3): 142–58.

Morrissey, S. (2010) "The economy of free and open source software in the preservation of digital artefacts," *Library Hi Tech*, 28(2): 211–23.

Mostad-Jensen, A. (2009) "The impact of economic recession on libraries: a past, present and future view," *Libreas: Library Ideas*, 5(5), available at *http://libreas.eu/ ausgabe14/007mos.htm.*

Mouritsen, J. (2009) "Classification, measurement and the ontology of intellectual capital entities," *Journal of Human Resource Costing & Accounting*, 13(2): 154–62.

Mouritsen, J., Larsen, H.T., and Bukh, P.N. (2001) "Valuing the future: intellectual capital supplements at Skandia," *Journal of Accounting, Auditing & Accountability*, 14(4): 399–422.

Mouritsen, J., Bukh, P.N., Flagstad, K., Thorbjornsen, S., Rosenkrands, N., Kotni, S., et al. (2003) (Danish Guidelines) "Intellectual Capital Statements—The New Guideline," Ministry of Science and Education Denmark, available at *http://en.vtu.dk/publications/2003/intellectual- capital-statements-the-new-guideline.*

Mullen, P. (2003) "Delphi: myths and reality," *Journal of Health Organization and Management*, 17(1): 37–52.

Mullins, J. (2001) "People-centered management in a library context," *Library Review*, 50(6): 305–9.

Nash, (1998) "Accounting for the future, a disciplined approach to value-added accounting," available at *http://home.sprintmail.com/~humphreynash/index.htm*.

Neely, A., Marr, B., Roos, G., Pike, St., and Gupta, O. (2003) "Towards the third generation of performance measurement," *Controlling*, 3/4: 129–35, available at *www.som.cranfield.ac.uk/som/dinamic-content/research/cbp/2003,%20Towards%203rd%20Generation%20 PM%20%28Controlling,%20Neely_Marr_Roos_Pike_ Gupta%29.pdf*.

Nelson, W. (1982) *Applied Data Life Analysis*, New York: John Wiley and Sons.

Nfila, R.B. and Drako-Ampem, W. (2002) "Developments in academic library consortia from the 1960s through to 2000: a review of the literature," *Library Management*, 23(4/5): 203–12.

Odlyzko, A. (1999) "Competition and cooperation: libraries and publishers in the transition to electronic scholarly journals," *The Journal of Electronic Publishing*, 4(4), available at *http://quod.lib.umich.edu/cgi/t/text/text-idx?c =jep;view=text;rgn=main;idno=3336451.0004.411*.

OECD (2003) *Glossary of Statistical Terms*, available at *http://stats.oecd.org/glossary/detail.asp?ID=1121*.

OECD (2005) *OECD Handbook on Economic Globalisation Indicators*, Paris, France: OECD.

Pacios, A. (2007) "The priorities of public libraries at the onset of the third millennium," *Library Management*, 28(6/7): 416–27.

Pankl, R.R. (2010) "Marketing the public library's business resources to small businesses," *Journal of Business & Finance Librarianship*, 15(2): 94–103.

Pember, M. (2002) "A decade of recordkeeping education at Curtin University of Technology: flux and flexibility, Australian Library and Information Association," *The*

Australian Library Journal, 52(1), available at *www.alia. org.au/publishing/alj/52.1/full.text/decade.recordkeeping. html*.

Peng, T.-J.A. (2011) "Resource fit in inter-firm partnership: intellectual capital perspective," *Journal of Intellectual Capital*, 12(1): 20–42.

Peters, D. and Lossau, N. (2011) "DRIVER: building a sustainable infrastructure for global repositories," *The Electronic Library*, 29(2): 249–60.

Poll, R. (2007) "Benchmarking with quality indicators: national projects," *Performance Measurement and Metrics*, 8(1): 41–53.

Pors, N.O. (2007) "Globalisation, culture and social capital: library professionals on the move," *Library Management*, 28(4/5): 181–90.

Porta, J.I.D. and Oliver, J.L.H. (2006) "How to measure IC in clusters: empirical evidence," *Journal of Intellectual Capital*, 7(3): 354–80.

Portugal, F.H. (2000) *Valuating Information Intangibles: Measuring the Bottom Line Contribution of Librarians and Information Professionals*, Washington, DC: Special Libraries Association.

Press, W.H., Flannery, B.P., Teukolsky, S.A., and Vetterling, W.T. (1986) *Numerical Recipes: The Art of Scientific Computing*, Cambridge: Cambridge University Press.

Pulic, A. (1997) "The physical and intellectual capital of Austrian banks," available at *http://irc.mcmaster.ca*.

Pulic, A. (1998) "Measuring the performance of intellectual potential in knowledge economy," available at *www. vaic-on.net*.

Pulic, A. (2000) "An accounting tool for IC management," available at *www.vaic-on.net*.

Pulic, A. (2004) "Basic information on VAIC™," available at *www.vaic-on.net*.

Ramirez, Y. (2010) "Intellectual capital models in the Spanish public sector," *Journal of Intellectual Capital*, 11(2): 248–64.

Reilly, R.F. and Schweihs, R.P. (1998) *Valuing Intangible Assets*, New York: McGraw-Hill.

Rodov, I. and Leliaert, P. (2002) "FiMIAM—Financial method of intangible assets measurement," *Journal of Intellectual Capital*, 3: 323–36.

Rooney-Browne, C. (2009) "Rising to the challenge: a look at the role of public libraries in times of recession," *Library Review*, 58(5): 341–52.

Roos, G., Pike, S., and Fernström, L. (2005) *Managing Intellectual Capital in Practice*, Oxford: Butterworth-Heinemann, Elsevier.

Roos, J., Roos, G., Edvinsson, L., and Dragonetti, N.C. (1997) *Intellectual Capital: Navigating in the New Business Landscape*, London: Macmillan.

Rowley, J. (1999) "What is Knowledge Management?," *Library Management*, 20(8): 416–19.

Saaty, T. (1990) *Multicriteria Decision Making: The Analytic Hierarchy Process*, Pittsburgh, PA: RWS Publications.

Sanchez, P., Elena, S., and Castrillo, R. (2009) "Intellectual capital dynamics in universities: a reporting model," *Journal of Intellectual Capital*, 10(2): 307–24.

Schiavone, F. and Simoni, M. (2011) "An experience-based view of co-opetition in R&D networks," *European Journal of Innovation Management*, 14(2): 136–54.

Schiuma, G. and Marr, B. (2001) "Managing knowledge in ebusinesses: the knowledge audit cycle," *Profit with People*, Deloitte & Touche.

Schiuma, G., Lerro, A., and Carlucci, D. (2008) "The Knoware Tree and the Regional Intellectual Capital Index: an assessment within Italy," *Journal of Intellectual Capital*, 9(2): 283–300.

Seavey, C. (2003) "The American public library during the great depression," *Library Review*, 52(8): 373–8.

Self, J. (2003) "From values to metrics: implementation of the balanced scorecard at a university library," *Performance Measurement and Metrics*, 4(2): 57–63.

Sheffer, C. (2008) "Escape from bad times," *Public Libraries*, 47(6): 6–16.

Sheng, X. and Sun, L. (2007) "Developing knowledge innovation culture of libraries," *Library Management*, 28(1/2): 36–52.

Sidorko, P.E. (2010) "Demonstrating RoI in the library: the Holy Grail search continues," *Library Management*, 31(8/9): 645–53.

Sidorko, P.E. and Yang, T.T. (2011) "Knowledge exchange and community engagement: an academic library perspective," *Library Management*, 32(6/7): 385–97.

Sirikrai, S. and Tang, J. (2006) "Industrial competitiveness analysis: using the analytic hierarchy process," *Journal of High Technology Management Research*, 17: 71–83.

Skandia Insurance Company (1995–2000) *Visualizing Intellectual Capital in Skandia: Supplement to Skandia Annual Reports 1994–2000*, Skandia Insurance Company, Stockholm, Sweden.

Skinner, K.R., Keats, B.J., and Zimmer, W.J. (2001) "A comparison of three estimators of the Weibull parameters," *Quality and Reliability Engineering International*, 17: 249–56.

Smith, K. (2011) "Researching the Information Commons (RIC)," *Library Hi Tech News*, 3: 20–4.

Stewart, T.A. (2001) "Intellectual capital: ten years later, how far we've come," *Fortune*, 143(11): 192–3.

Stewart, T.A. (1997) *Intellectual Capital: The New Wealth of Organizations*, New York: Doubleday/Currency.

Stolowy, H. and Cazavan, A.J. (2001) "International accounting disharmony: the case of intangibles," *Accounting, Auditing & Accountability Journal*, 14(4): 477–96.

Stopper, M. and Salais, R. (1997) *Worlds of Production*, London: Harvard University Press.

Streveler, R.A., Olds, B.M., Miller, R.L., and Nelson, M.A. (2003) "Using a Delphi study to identify the most difficult concepts for students to master in thermal and transport science," in *Proceedings of the 2003 American Society for Engineering Education Annual Conference & Exposition*, Session 2430.

Sullivan, P. (2000) *Value-driven Intellectual Capital: How to Convert Intangible Corporate Assets into Market Value*, Hoboken, NJ: John Wiley & Sons.

Sullivan, P.H. Jr and Sullivan, P.H. Sr (2000) "Valuing intangible companies—an intellectual capital approach," *Journal of Intellectual Capital*, 1(4): 328–40.

Sveiby, K.E. (1997a) *The Invisible Balance Sheet: Key Indicators for Accounting, Control and Evaluation of Know-How Companies*, Stockholm: Konrad Group.

Sveiby, K.E. (1997b) *The New Organizational Wealth: Managing and Measuring Knowledge Based Assets*, Berrett-Koehler, San Francisco, CA. The chapter on measuring intangibles, available at *www.sveiby.com/articles/MeasureIntangibleAssets.html*.

Sveiby, K.E. (2010) *Methods for Measuring Intangible Assets*, available at *www.sveiby.com/articles/IntangibleMethods.htm*.

Talukdar, A. (2008) *What is Intellectual Capital? And Why it Should be Measured*, Attainix Consulting Report, available at *www.attainix.com/Downloads/WhatIsIntellectualCapital.pdf*.

Todd, R.J. and Southon, G. (2001) "Educating for a knowledge management future: perceptions of library and information professionals," *The Australian Library Journal*, 50(4), available at *www.alia.org.au/publishing/alj/50.4/full.text/educating.html*.

Town, J.S. (2010) "Value, impact and the transcendent library: progress and pressures in performance measurement and evaluation," Keynote speaker of 2010 Library Assessment Conference: *Building Effective, Sustainable, Practical Assessment*, Baltimore, USA.

Train, B. and Elkin, J. (2001) "Measuring the unmeasurable: reader development and its impact on performance measurement of the public sector," *Library Review*, 50(6): 295–404.

Ulvik, S. (2010) "Why should the library collect immigrants' memories? A study of a multicultural memory group at a public library in Oslo," *New Library World*, 111(3/4): 154–60.

Uzoka, F.M.E. and Ijatuyi, O.A. (2005) "Decision support system for library acquisitions: a framework," *The Electronic Library*, 23(4): 453–62.

Vaidya, O. and Kumar, S. (2006) "Analytic hierarchy process: an overview of applications," *European Journal of Operational Research*, 169: 1–29.

van Deventer, M.J. (2002) "Introducing intellectual capital management in an information support services," Ph.D. thesis, Faculty of Humanities, University of Pretoria, available at *http://upetd.up.ac.za/thesis/available/etd-08012003-162454/unrestricted/00front.pdf*.

Varheim, A. (2009) "Public libraries: places creating social capital?," *Library Hi Tech*, 27(3): 372–81.

Vasconcelos, A.C. (2008) "Dilemmas in knowledge management," *Library Management*, 29(4/5): 422–43.

Vasconcelos, A., Ellis, D., Pieter, L., and Chavda, A. (2001) "Problems in the measurement of intellectual assets," in *Proceedings of the Second European Conference on*

Knowledge Management, pp. 705–20, Bled, Slovenia: Bled School of Management.

Walden, G.R. (2006) "Focus group interviewing in the library literature: a selective annotated bibliography 1996–2005," *Reference Services Review,* 34(2): 222–41.

Walton, G. (2007) "Theory, research and practice in library management 2: the balanced product portfolio," *Library Management,* 28(4/5): 262–8.

White, L.N. (2007a) "Unseen measures: the need to account for intangibles," *Bottom Line: Managing Library Finances,* 20(2): 77–84.

White, L.N. (2007b) "A kaleidoscope of possibilities: strategies for assessing human capital in libraries," *Bottom Line: Managing Library Finances,* 20(3): 109–15.

White, L.N. (2008) "Aligning library assessment processes to the library's service environment: a conceptual model," *Library Review,* 57(7): 499–513.

Woodsworth, A. (2005) "Two million dollars times three," *Bottom Line: Managing Library Finances,* 18(3): 126–32.

Zhang, W. (2006) "Digital library intellectual property right evaluation and method," *The Electronic Library,* 25(3): 267–73.

Index

Printed and bound by CPI Group (UK) Ltd, Croydon, CR0 4YY

08/05/2025

01864973-0002